D1600621

To Martin Dillon
in appreciation of
his interest and
guidance, with
best wishes
Salma Jayyusi
November 17, 2009

MODERN ARABIC LITERATURE IN TRANSLATION

Salih J. Altoma

MODERN ARABIC LITERATURE IN TRANSLATION

A Companion

SAQI

British Library Cataloguing-in-Publication Data
A catalogue record for this book is available from the British Library

ISBN 0 86356 597 2
EAN 9-780863-565977

This edition first published 2005

SAQI
26 Westbourne Grove
London W2 5RH
www.saqibooks.com

To Amal, Tiba and Reef
in appreciation of their understanding and support

Contents

Acknowledgments 9
A Note on Transliteration and Footnotes 10
Introduction 11

1. Translating Najib Mahfuz: His Place in American Publications 21
    Arabic as a 'Linguistic Iron Curtain' 22
    Mahfuz in American Publications 26
    Bibliography 30
        Part I: Pre-1988 Publications 31
        Part II: Since 1988 41

2. Arabic Fiction, 1947–2003: 54
    1947–1967 54
    1968–1988 55
    1988–2003 57

3. Arabic Fiction in English Translation:
    A Chronological Bibliography, 1947–2003 61
    Arabic Works in International Anthologies 91
    Authors Index 93
    Women Novelists 97
    Translators Index 98
    Titles Index 103
    Publishers Index 113
    Countries Index 118

4. Arabic Poetry: An Overview of Selected Anthologies 119
    Bibliography 126

Contents

Pan-Arab Anthologies   126
Selected Regional Anthologies   127
Selected Anthologies of Poets   129

5. Arabic Poetry in International Anthologies:
    A Partial but Positive Representation   134
       Bibliography   138

6. Arabic Drama   151
    Bibliography   155
       Anthologies and Collected Works   155
       Individual Works   157

APPENDIX: Literary Autobiographies and Memoirs   161
    Selected Interviews   163
    Studies   164

Acknowledgments

This is book is the outcome of several years of teaching and research in the field of modern Arabic literature. As its various chapters indicate, it required consulting countless books most of which were made accessible to me through the services of the Document Delivery (Interlibrary Loan) Department at the Main Library of Indiana University. I wish to gratefully acknowledge my indebtedness to the staff of this department for their prompt and positive response to my seemingly endless interlibrary loan requests. I am also indebted to the Reference Librarians and to Mark Day, the Middle East area librarian for the advice, bibliographical guidance, and assistance they have extended to me over the years.

I owe a special debt of gratitude to Mona Lababidi Khateeb who assisted me generously with her technical expertise and guidance in preparing this book for publication.

The book includes material published earlier as essay in the following publications: *The Yearbook of Comparative and General Literature, Translation Review,* and the *Encyclopedia of Literary Translation into English.* I wish to thank their editors for their interest in my work and their permission to incorporate in this book the previously published material.

A Note on Transliteration and Footnotes

I have followed the transliteration system of WorldCat/OCLC(Online Computer Library Center) in transliterating the Arabic names of authors: e.g. Gamal Ghitany = Jamal Ghitani, Mohamed Berrada = Muhammad Baradah. No diacritical marks are used except the marks for hamzah ' and 'ayn '. In the case of translators, I have kept the same spelling they use in their publications. In general, bibliographical references are given in parentheses within the text of each chapter. Footnotes are provided in cases that require additional information or more details.

Introduction

In reading much of what has been written on Arabic literature in translation one cannot miss the many comments made about its state in the West.[1] There are too many examples to mention here, but it may be instructive to cite a few that represent a wide range of relevant issues.[2]

---

1. The use of the term 'West' here and in other contexts may be inaccurate or misleading in view of the book's focus on English and the Anglo–American world. No attempt is made to discuss the translation of Arabic literature in other European languages although related studies suggest certain similar problems. See, for example, the following studies or surveys: Maria Luz Comendador et al., 'The Translation of Contemporary Arabic Literature into Spanish', *Yearbook of Comparative and General Literature (YCGL)* 48 (2000): 115–125; Hartmut Fähndrich, 'Viewing the 'Orient' and Translating its Literature in the Shadow of *The Arabian Nights*', *YCGL* 48 (2000): 95–106; Richard Jacquemond, 'Translation and Cultural Hegemony: The Case of French– Arabic Translation', *Rethinking Translation: Discourse, Subjectivity, Ideology*, ed. Lawrence Venuti. New York: Routledge, 1992: 139-158; Monica Ruocco, 'A Survey of Translations and Studies on Arabic Literature Published in Italy (1987–1997)', *Arabic and Middle Eastern Literatures* 3.1 (2000): 63–73; and Marina Stagh, 'The Translation of Contemporary Arabic Literature into Swedish', *YCGL* 48 (2000): 107–114.

2. Some of the sources are given in the text. For the others see Hosam Aboul-Ela, 'Challenging the Embargo: Arabic Literature in the US Market', *Middle East Report* (Summer 2001): 42–44; Elizabeth Warnock Fernea, 'Another Measure of Iraq: Without an Alphabet, Without a Face: Saadi Youssef' [Book review], *Los Angeles Times* January 4, 2004, Part R: 12; Peter Clark, *Arabic Literature Unveiled: Challenges of Translation* Durham, UK: University of Durham, Durham Middle East Paper No. 63, 2000: 13–14; Tayeb Salih, interview by Mohammed Shaheen, *Banipal* 10/11 (Summer 2001): 82–84; Sarah Maguire's remark is reported in 'Translating Literature and Poetry', *Banipal* 3 (October 1998): 75; Mursi Saad El-Din, 'Hall of Mirrors', *Al-Ahram Weekly Online* 3–9 February 2000. This article provides a summary of the remarks made by the panellists on the issue of translating modern Arabic literature into English. The seminar itself, held in Cairo, was

(continued...)

I don't think that enough Arabic literature is translated. There is some interest in fiction, some novels have been translated into English, French, German, etc., but to a limited extent. (Tayeb Salih 2001)

Arab literature is still largely the preserve of Middle Eastern specialists. It has not come out of the ghetto. (Peter Clark 2000)

I am concerned by the quality of some of the Arabic–English translations, which I have occasion to look at in much detail as I teach a course on Arabic novels in translation … Even undergraduate students who aren't specialists in language mock the language in some of them. (Catherine Cobham, quoted in *Cairo Times* 6–12 December 2000)

Most translations of contemporary Arab poets such as Mahmoud Darwish and Adonis are very bad. (Sarah Maguire, quoted in *Banipal* 1998)

The nature of language, he [Anthony Calderbank] said, makes translating an ultimately frustrating endeavour. (Mursi Saad El-Din 2000)

Eleven years have passed since Edward Said's polemic in *The Nation* exposed the dominating US book market's prejudice against Arabic literature, but Said's words remain depressingly relevant today … the 1988 award to Naguib Mahfouz has been little more than an obstacle to younger Arab writers and their translators in their attempts to get the attention of self-satisfied publishers. (Hosam Aboul Ela 2001)

The number of Arab writers translated into English is still minimal, and the same names (Nawal al-Sadaawi, for example) seem to be chosen over and over again, perhaps because her works appeal to and confirm certain stereotypes the West holds of the Arab world … (Magda al-Nowaihi, quoted in *Cairo Times* 6–12 December 2000)

Such concerns, often expressed by translators and authors of Arabic works, are undoubtedly legitimate, and they do indicate that there are still problems that impede the promotion of Arabic literature. However, they are largely based on

(...continued)
    organized by the American University in Cairo Press. See also on the same subject Daniel Rolph, 'Crisis in the Art of Arabic Translation', *Middle East Times* No.7 (2000).

personal impressions or partial familiarity with the field. Certain remarks regarding the quality of translations from Arabic are vague or general and fail almost totally to refer to what has actually been translated, whether before or after 1988, the year Najib Mahfuz was awarded the Nobel Prize for Literature. Those who voice such views do not seem to take into account the vast body of literature that has been translated since the 1950s or the positive progress that Arabic literature has made in reaching a relatively wider audience in recent decades – not only readers or reviewers of printed Arabic books, but also unconventional readers who access the Internet to pursue their interest in Arabic literature or other fields. Even a cursory search of the Internet will reveal how visible and accessible modern Arabic literature has become to readers throughout the world, and how the Internet itself has turned into a potent medium of instant information, which can effectively serve up Arabic or other 'embargoed' literature.

Such comments often overlook the two-fold question I mentioned earlier; namely what has been translated from modern Arabic literature into English during the last fifty years? And what has been accomplished in terms of translations and reviews since 1988 when Mahfuz won the Nobel Prize?

Other important questions related to the readership in the West deserve serious consideration. Who are the people who read Arabic literature in translation? Do they include any segments (small as they may be) of Arab/Muslim communities, who run into millions in the United States or other Western countries? Do Europeans and Americans of Arab background read about their Arab literary or cultural heritage? Do they acquire books or subscribe to journals dealing with Arabic literature? The latter is obviously significant because of its relevance to marketing Arabic books and to its potential impact on the attitude of commercial publishers towards translations from Arabic. This issue is also relevant to what Edward Said described as 'the absence of an Arab cultural intervention in the world debate', although he referred only to 'Arab writers, their publishing houses, ministries of culture and embassies in Western capitals'.[1]

It is with the first basic question in mind that I sought to prepare this book on the translation of modern Arabic literature into English since 1947. It should be viewed primarily, if not only, as a guide to the countless translations that have been published between 1947 and 2003, although other relevant issues are briefly discussed in different chapters.

The guide covers only translations published as books. Other translated works published in journals and newspapers or on the Internet are generally excluded, except for a small number related to drama and autobiographical

---

1. Edward Said, 'Embargoed Literature', *The Nation* September 17, 1990: 280.

texts. Such translations are too many to be listed in one volume and their sources, with the exception of the Internet are not easily accessible.[1]

The period before 1947 is not included because it witnessed a few isolated – perhaps no more than five – books of translations representing drama and fiction. I have in mind works such as Taha Husayn's *An Egyptian Childhood* (London 1932) translated by E. H. Paxton and his *The Stream of Days* (Cairo 1943) translated by Hillary Wayment; Ahmad Shawqi's play *Majnun Layla* (Cairo 1933) translated by Arthur Arberry; and Mahmud Kamil's *Blue Wings and Other Stories* (Cairo 1941) translated by G. Brackenbury. Other pre-1947 works written originally in English include *At Random: Thoughts on Humanism* by Ahmad Zaki Abu Shadi (Abushady) (Alexandria, Egypt 1937) and *Abushady the Poet: A Critical Study* (Leipzig 1938) by I. A. Edham. This is in marked contrast to the greater number of works by the Mahjar (émigré writers) group in the United States, such as Jubran Khalil Jubran (Gibran), Mikha'il Nu'aymah (Naimy) and Amin al-Rihani, who were more accessible in English than their compatriots in the Arab world.[2]

While working on this project, I made every effort over the years to include, as comprehensively as possible, translations published not only in English-speaking countries (the United States, Great Britain, Canada, Australia, India) but also in different Arab countries.

The obvious reason for focusing also on Arab translation efforts is that for almost a century Arab writers and institutions have advocated and sought to execute a number of projects in support of translation from and into Arabic.

---

1. For earlier efforts covering both books and periodical items, see the following:

Roger Allen and Michael Hillmann, 'Arabic Literature in English Translation', *Literature East and West* 25 (1989): 104–116.
Salih Altoma, *Modern Arabic Literature: A Bibliography of Articles, Books, Dissertations, and Translations in English* Bloomington: Asian Studies Research Institute, Indiana University, 1975.
—— *Modern Arabic Poetry in English Translation: A Bibliography*. Tangier: The King Fahd School of Translation, 1993.
Mohammad Bakir Alwan, 'A Bibliography of Modern Arabic Fiction in English Translation', *Middle East Journal* 26 (1972): 195–200.
—— 'A Bibliography of Modern Arabic Poetry in English Translation', *Middle East Journal* 27 (1973): 373–381.
Margaret Anderson, *Arabic Materials in English Translation: A Bibliography of Works from the pre-Islamic Period to 1977* Boston: G. K. Hall, 1980: 180–207 on 'Modern Arabic Literature.'
Ragai N. Makai, *Modern Arabic Literature: A Bibliography* Lanham, MD: Scarecrow Press, 1998.

2. For more bibliographical information on the place of Mahjar literature in English, see Makai (1998: 125–130), Altoma (1975:45–56) and his bibliography 'Arabic–Western Literary Relations in American Publications', *Yearbook of Comparative and General Literature* 48 (2000): 255–257.

Central among their objectives has been to promote a better understanding of their national aspirations and their cultural heritage, particularly in Western countries. Since as long ago as the 1920s, Arab writers and scholars have felt that their literature was ignored, distorted or marginalized in the West. Consequently, they took an active role in translating into English (and other European languages) the works they regarded as representative of their literary achievements. Reference in the literature is often made to *rawa'i'* (masterpieces) of Arabic literature and their translations. As a result (or as a by-product) of this interest, numerous translations (perhaps more than the 170 indicated in the following chapters) have been undertaken mostly by native speakers of Arabic. Egypt has led the way in this area but other Arab countries (Iraq, Jordan, Lebanon, United Arab Emirates and others) have also taken part in such efforts, not to mention numerous Arab writers and scholars living in Western countries. This large number of such translations, incomplete or partial as it is, serves to demonstrate the extent of Arabs' involvement in translating their literature in their effort to promote a better understanding of their culture. It also raises a number of questions that have not yet been answered, whether in relation to the literary merits of the works selected for translation, the quality of the translations themselves or their success in reaching their intended Western audience beyond the Arab world. Indeed, commentators have recently gone so far as to question the wisdom of certain initiatives on the part of Arab translators.[1] Without a thorough and systematic study of the Arab-sponsored translations, it is difficult to judge their effectiveness in promoting Arabic culture and literature in Western countries. Most, if not all, of the translations are made accessible to specialists or general readers through libraries that acquire them in the United States or other Western countries. They may reach non-Arabic-speaking residents in different Arab countries or other foreign visitors.[2] *There is, however, no indication that they reach a wide audience in the West or are effective in attracting more readers. In addition, they are rarely cited, not even briefly, in book reviews except in several isolated notices published by specialists.* By making these observations, I do not intend to question the value of Arab initiatives to promote their literature. They are not only

---

1. Elie Chalala, 'Poet and Critic Nouri Jarah [Jarrah] Laments Standards of Arab Literary Criticism. Rushing Poetry into Translation', *aljadid* No. 34 (Winter 2001): 3, 11, 15, 23. Jarrah, according to Chalala, has his reservations about state-sponsored projects and in particular the rush to translate Arabic poetry into English and other European languages. He seems to suggest that many of the translations distort the image of Arab poetry in general.

2. We have no way of documenting how foreign residents react to such locally produced translations, although in 1968 Stanley Post, in an article entitled 'Notes on Modern Egyptian Short Stories' (*Critique* 11 (1968): 20–24), characterized some of the authors he read in translation (Taha Husayn, Tawfiq al-Hakim, Abbas al-Aqqad, etc.) as 'totally unreadable' and added other extremely negative observations.

legitimate but also necessary in view of the relentless campaign being waged in different forms and channels against the Arabs and their culture and of the deplorable state of ignorance or prejudice prevalent among large segments of the population in the United States and other Western countries. It is also important to stress that Arab cultural and literary initiatives are not unique. Other nations, including the United States and Japan, have been engaged in similar projects.[1] However, for Arab initiatives to succeed they must be re-evaluated in light of their past performance and accomplishments. Among the most basic issues to be addressed in such an evaluation are the criteria and procedures by which particular works or authors are selected for translation. Do they really represent the best and most potentially appealing works that Arabic literature has to offer? How are translators selected? Where are the works published? Arab initiatives that have relied primarily on native translators have evidently had limited success. To be more effective, more qualified translators in the target language should be involved in translating Arabic literature, whether they work alone or in cooperation with equally qualified native speakers. As far as the place of publication outside the Arab world is concerned, constructive efforts should be made to select and support publishers willing to publish and market translations from Arabic. As the chapter on fiction indicates, major publishers have only recently been engaged in the publication of Arabic works, and to a limited extent. In collecting the data presented in the various chapters, I have relied on several American and European library sources or bibliographies: Index Islamicus, The Library of Congress, WorldCat/OCLC (Online Computer Library Center), RLIN (Research Libraries Information Network), MLA (Modern Language Association), PCI (Periodicals Contents Index) and the UNESCO's *Index*

1. Reference should be made to the US-sponsored Franklin Book Programs (1952–1978), which aimed at translating and publishing American books in Arab and other Middle Eastern countries. More recently (2003–2004), Professor Juan Cole (of the University of Michigan) has established The 'Americana in Arabic' Translation Program. The programme seeks to translate into Arabic important American books and to subsidize their publication and distribution, on the grounds that, as Cole says, 'the classics of American thought and literature have been little translated into Arabic'. Another noteworthy programme is The Japanese Literature Publishing Project, which aims to translate and disseminate abroad works of modern Japanese literature. The project is guided by a number of criteria regarding the selection of books, translators and publishers. Books should have earned a 'stable reputation' in Japan and have the potential to appeal to foreign readers. Translators are to be chosen on the basis of their combined competence in and grasp of both Japanese and the target languages and their cultures. Translated works are to be published and marketed by publishers in foreign countries. For more details regarding these and other important criteria see Kizuki Chiaki, 'Sense and Sensibility', *Look Japan* 48.562 (January 2003): 36–38 or www.lookjapan.com (January 2003/Culture Feature).

Translationum Database.[1] They proved to be extremely helpful in identifying and verifying nearly all the translations (about 460) listed in the guide. Although a large number of translations published in the Arab world have been identified, I have no doubt that there are other works that I have not been able to verify or identify for a number of reasons. Among them is the lack of updated reliable Arabic sources or databases on this subject or in other fields, as confirmed by a recent study (April 2004) on electronic databases at Arab universities.[2]

The guide as it stands now has a number of limitations in terms of its scope and coverage. Of the Mahjar group, it includes only Nu'aymah, who spent most of his life in Lebanon from the 1930s onwards. It focuses primarily on the three main genres of drama, fiction (novels and short stories) and poetry. Apart from a few autobiographical novels, which are listed under fiction, autobiographical works are excluded, mainly because only a few of what I call literary or 'belletristic' autobiographies or autobiographical writings have been translated. I use the terms 'literary' or 'belletristic' here in a narrow sense to refer specifically to diverse accounts written by poets, novelists and playwrights. However, I have made a preliminary attempt to identify (see the Appendix at the end of the book) translations of such accounts as well as selected studies. I have included several interviews with leading Arab novelists and poets, mostly published in *Banipal*, because they provide illuminating autobiographical information as well as views regarding the translation of Arabic literature.

The guide also does not cover works written originally in English or translated into English from other languages, even if they appeared in Arabic after their initial publication. Note for example *The Belt* by Ahmed Abodehamn (Ahmad Abu Dahman; London: Saqi; St Paul, MN: Ruminator Books, 2002). It is not included because it was originally written and published in French (2000) before it was translated into English by Nadia Benabid, although it

---

1. It should be noted that literary translations published in Arab countries are rarely cited in the UNESCO's Index Translationum Database. Out of 1,066 records found in the database, only a small number represent translations published in an Arab country. The notable exception is the coverage given to Saddam Hussein's translated speeches or works (which exceed sixty titles) and a few Iraqi literary works. For an informative analysis of trends and attitudes regarding translation and 'the exercise of colonial power' in the selection of works to be translated, see Vaiju Naravane, 'Fifty Years of Translation: *The Index Translationum* Completes a Half Century', *Publishing Research Quarterly* 15.4 (Winter 1999/2000): 23–38. Note the list of more than a hundred widely translated authors (35–38). It includes no modern Arab author apart from Khalil Gibran.

2. According to the author of this study (Reima al-Jarf) who surveyed the home pages of 202 Arab universities, Arab databases are still lacking. See her article 'Availability and Use of Electronic Databases at Arab Universities', www.arabicwata.org [World Arabic Translators Association] April 13, 2004.

appeared in Arabic as well under the title *al-Hizam* (Beirut: Saqi, 2001, 2002). *Menstruation*, the novel by the Syrian writer Ammar Abdulhamid (Abd al-Hamid; London: Saqi, 2001) and *Fatma: A Novel of Arabia* by Raja Alem are other cases in point. A noted Saudi woman novelist and playwright, Alem (Alim) chose to write *Fatma* in English in cooperation with the American writer Tom McDonough (Syracuse, NY: Syracuse University Press, 2001). Many other similar works (novels, diaries, autobiographies, books of verse) have been published in English, especially in recent years. They deserve undoubtedly to be considered as a subject of a separate survey or study.

As the Table of Contents indicates, the book is divided into six chapters covering Najib Mahfuz in American publications, fiction, poetry, the place of poetry in international anthologies, and drama. The chapter on Najib Mahfuz is added because his itinerary in the West provides an illustration of the issues and obstacles that are relevant to the translation of modern Arabic literature in general. It discusses the role of publishers, the negative attitude still prevalent in Western countries, the difficulties attributed to the Arabic language and the tendency to judge Arabic literary works by Western criteria.

The second chapter, dealing with fiction, identifies briefly three stages, which reflect the gradual progress made in the translation of Arabic novels and short stories: 1947–1967, 1968–1988 and since 1988. The translations are numbered (from 1 to 322) and are listed in Chapter Three in alphabetical order under the year of their publication between 1947 and 2003. As will be readily noted, out of 322 translations listed, about 200 were published after 1988, the year Najib Mahfuz was awarded the Nobel Prize for Literature. This fact alone underlines at least the relatively increased visibility that Arabic literature has attained, if not a notable shift in Western attitudes towards Arabic literature. There are other positive trends, such as the numerous reviews or brief notices that appear in general periodicals and mainstream newspapers in the United States. The other important trend is reflected in the number of editions published in certain cases. Note for example Tayeb Salih's *Season of Migration to the North*, which was reissued at least nine times since its first edition in 1969. We also notice that Arabic works began to appear since 1990 in several international anthologies, although there is still a tendency to exclude, for one reason or another, selections from Arabic.[1]

The chapter also deals with the role of different publishers in supporting translations from Arabic, the increasing number of Arab women novelists and

---

1. As an example, see *A World of Short Stories: 18 short stories from Around the World* Ed. Yvonne Collioud Sisko. New York: Longman, 2004. Intended for college readers, the anthology excludes the whole Middle East region, but it covers Africa (non-Arab countries), Asia (China, India, Korea, Malaysia), and other Western regions. More examples are cited in Chapter Five on Arabic Poetry in International Anthologies.

the uneven geographical representation of authors from different Arab countries.

In dealing with poetry, I have focused on several pan-Arab anthologies published between 1950 and 2001. They include Salma Jayyusi's highly regarded and most representative anthology, *Modern Arabic Poetry* (1987), and two anthologies of poetry by Arab women: Kamal Boullata's pioneering work *Women of the Fertile Crescent* (1981) and the more comprehensive anthology entitled *The Poetry of Arab Women* edited by Nathalie Handal (2001). Both anthologies cover translations of poems written originally in French and other Western languages. The anthologies or collections are listed under three headings: Pan-Arab Anthologies, Regional Anthologies and Anthologies of Individual Poets.

The place of Arabic literature in anthologies of world literature has not been adequately considered by writers concerned with the dissemination of Arabic literature, in spite of the fact that international anthologies serve as a useful forum to introduce Arabic or other national literatures to a large audience. As such anthologies are widely used by both academic and general audiences, I have chosen to discuss in a separate chapter (Chapter Five) the extent of recognition or representation that modern Arabic poetry has attained in recent years. Although the chapter indicates that tangible progress has been made towards greater representation of Arabic poetry, it also points to cases that either completely exclude Arabic poetry or limit its representation for political or other reasons.

The final chapter briefly outlines the history of Arabic drama and the relative paucity of English translations of it, largely because of its peculiar development as a new genre in Arabic. Compared with the many translations of fiction and poetry, drama has had thus far a limited appeal beyond a largely Arabist audience. As the bibliography indicates, most of the plays listed have been published in Egypt, which may explain in part the drama's limited circulation.

CHAPTER ONE

Translating Najib Mahfuz: His Place in American Publications

Najib Mahfuz (also known as Naguib Mahfouz; b. Cairo, 1911 or 1912, BA in Philosophy, Cairo University, 1934) is rightly credited with the primary role in developing the novel in Arabic as a new genre within a relatively short period. Having dedicated himself to the art of fiction since the 1930s, Mahfuz has managed to emulate many of the Western fictional techniques, styles and trends and to create, in the process, a distinctly Arabic narrative art. By the mid-1950s, when his magnum opus, *The Trilogy* (translated as *Palace Walk*, *Palace of Desire* and *Sugar Street*), was published, Mahfuz had attained the status of a literary landmark, hailed not only in Egypt but also throughout the Arab world. As a noted Egyptian novelist said, 'You cannot picture Egypt without the Pyramids, nor can you conceive of Arabic literature without Naguib Mahfouz' (Kessler: 60).

Since that time, students of the Arabic novel, both Arabs and non-Arabs, have voiced general unanimity in this regard. Writing in 1963, Trevor LeGassick observed that in recent years Mahfuz's works 'have been showered with praise by the best critics of Arabic literature', and cited as an example Taha Husayn's review of *Bayn al-qasrayn* (*Palace Walk*), the first part of Mahfuz's trilogy. Husayn (1889–1973), known as the doyen of Arabic literature, summed up his praise by declaring, 'I do not doubt that this novel can stand comparison with the work of whatever international novelists you like to name in any language at all'(LeGassick 1963: 34). While George Sfeir (1966, 1968) refers to the trilogy's affinity with the tradition of Galsworthy's *The Forsyte Saga* or Thomas Mann's *Buddenbrooks*, the British Arabist William Cowan (1968: 172–173) presents Mahfuz as the greatest Arab novelist, ' ... in the grand style of Zola and Balzac, but who owes nothing to these two, being completely Egyptian' and a twentieth-century successor 'to those who gave us

The Thousand and One Nights. In her study of Yahya Haqqi, Miriam Cooke (138) likewise describes Mahfuz as 'the doyen of the novel in the entire Arabic-speaking world' and provides us with incidental remarks indicating Mahfuz's prominent position among other leading writers.

Of all scholars and critics listed in the bibliography, it is, perhaps, Roger Allen who should be recognized for his most influential role in presenting Mahfuz to his American readers as a great novelist. Allen's endeavours, which span more than twenty years (as shown in both parts of the bibliography), may be viewed as an important factor leading to the Nobel Committee's decision of 1988. What is especially noteworthy is that he presented Mahfuz as his first choice for the Nobel Prize only a few months before the decision was announced. Allen's second choice was the leading poet Adonis (Ali Ahmad Sa'id), whose name has been frequently cited as a possible candidate for the prize. As the Swedish author Kjell Espmark observes in his book *The Nobel Prize in Literature* (1991: 158), Allen's essay 'Arabic Literature and the Nobel Prize', which was published in the spring of 1988, 'turned out to be prophetic' and his nomination 'reads like a justification several months in advance for a choice that, in the usual way, was prepared for over the course of several years. Allen sums up Mahfuz's unique contribution as a great pioneer in terms that have become by now familiar and rather repetitious:

> He [Mahfuz] is recognized as the Arab world's leading writer of fiction because he has not only produced a whole stream of excellent novels over a period of four decades, but also turned the novel, as a means of societal comment and criticism, into an accessible and accomplished medium. His is a nomination which, the normalities of Arab politics aside, would be welcomed throughout the Arab world. (203)

In spite of the obvious unanimity over Mahfuz's stature as a man of letters, he remained, like other major Arab writers, largely unknown until 1988 except to a very limited Western (including American) readership. One of the reasons cited for the dearth of translations from Mahfuz's works or from modern Arabic literature in general is the Arabic language itself.

Arabic as a 'Linguistic Iron Curtain'

The Arabic language itself is often blamed not only for the slow progress of translation but also for other ills, including the West's failure to understand the Arab world or its culture. Arabic is variously described as a 'hurdle', 'a linguistic impasse' and 'a highly imprecise', 'ornate' or 'florid' language. In a long article on Mahfuz in *The New York Times Magazine* 3 June 1990, Brad Kessler suggests, for instance, that, 'the problem for English readers comes with the language', which is ' hard to render into English or the Romance languages'. He even finds Mahfuz's greatly simplified use of Arabic (regarded by many as a significant contribution) to be 'florid' and roughly equivalent to Shakespearean English. Furthermore, he refers to unnamed scholars who talk about 'a linguistic Iron Curtain', which separates Arabic literature from that of the West (62). Perhaps Kessler was echoing what John Fowles had stated earlier (1978) in his introduction to Najib Mahfuz's novel *Miramar*. Fowles does provide a fairly accurate and informative description of the difficulties arising in part from the dichotomy between the two varieties of Arabic and certain stylistic conventions. However, he needlessly blames Arabic for the West's failure adequately to understand Egypt or the Arab world, saying: 'This linguistic Iron Curtain has kept us miserably short of first-hand information about the very considerable changes that Egypt has undergone in this century' (viii).

Fowles seems to overlook the fact that language difficulties are not confined to Arabic (Chinese, Japanese and Russian have their own difficult features) and that such difficulties have not deterred genuinely serious students of Arabic or other languages from undertaking countless translations.

There are many other writers who likewise tend to perpetuate the notion that Arabic is an 'enormously evocative and enormously vague language' and a barrier that has kept 'much of Arab culture hidden from the West' or has kept the West ill-informed about modern Arabic literature or other matters concerning the Arab world (Dickey 1991; Horwitz 1991; Roberts 1993; Viorst 1994).

> As recently as 2000, a panellist in a seminar held in Cairo on the issue of translating modern Arabic literature into English was quoted as saying, 'the nature of language makes translating an ultimately frustrating endeavour' (Mursi Saad El-Din 2000).[1]

The negative remarks common in today's Western writings are less extreme than earlier statements. For example, the British historian George Young, in his book *Egypt* (London: 1927), not content with describing Arabic as the

---

1. Mursi Saad El-Din, 'Hall of Mirrors', *Al-Ahram Weekly Online* 3–9 February 2000. This article provides a summary of the remarks made by the panelists about translating modern Arabic literature into English. The seminar, held in Cairo, was organized by the American University in Cairo Press.

'most difficult of literary languages', greatly hampering literary expression, went on to predict its possible demise as Egypt's national language, writing: '*It is not impossible that in the distant future Egypt will substitute French for Arabic as other future nations of North Africa are already doing*' (284; emphasis is mine). Young's prediction was based on the premise that, 'as Europeanization develops and Islam declines, Arabic becomes more and more unsuitable as a medium of expression' (284). With notions such as these in mind, Edward Said's defence of Arabic (1988) is welcome. Said refers to its 'uniquely contested position in modern culture, defended and extolled by its native speakers and writers, belittled, attacked or ignored by foreigners for whom it has represented a last defended bastion of Arabism and Islam' (10).[1]

However, even today some Arab writers tend to exaggerate the difficulty of Arabic. In her 1988 essay on Mahfuz, 'A Genius for Synthesis', Ahdaf Soueif, an acclaimed and highly regarded novelist in English, makes an excellent case for Mahfuz's contribution to Arabic literature and language on the grounds of his extraordinary skill in bridging the distance between the written and spoken varieties of Arabic. But her remark that, 'Arabic is notorious for the vast chasm'[2] sounds too dramatic; it is inconsistent with the linguistic modifications or changes that have brought both varieties closer to each other, whether in daily use or works of literature, especially in fiction and drama. Other Arab accounts recently published in Britain and the United States offer a pessimistic view of the language situation in the Arab world. Writing in the *Chronicle of Higher Education* (August 2001), Daniel del Castillo cites remarks attributed to an Arab publisher who maintains that 'fewer and fewer people have an acceptable knowledge of this [Arabic] language' and goes as far as to declare, 'I think Arabic is a dead language, and we are witnessing the birth of several Arabic languages.'[3] A later article, which appeared in the *Manchester Guardian Weekly* (March 2004), likewise laments the Arabic language situation under the headline 'Arabic Teaching at Crisis Point', citing a video presentation that demonstrates the inability of Arab jobseekers (interviewed for a professional position) to 'sustain a conversation entirely in Arabic'. Other examples are presented to warn against ignoring the state of decline in Arabic teaching. But the article offers a well-balanced and less pessimistic view of Arabic and ends on the following hopeful note: 'In reality a new approach to

---

1. See also Said's eloquent defence of Arabic in 'Living in Arabic' *Raritan* 21.4 (Spring 2002): 220–236. Said dismisses contemporary complaints about Arabic as having no substance by such writers as Thomas Friedman and Bernard Lewis or some Arabs working in the West. He regards their knowledge and active use of the language as superficial or nonexistent.
2. Ahdaf Soueif, 'A Genius for Synthesis', *Times Literary Supplement* (21 October 1988): 1174.
3. See Castillo's article, 'The Arabic Publishing Scene', *Chronicle of Higher Education* (August 10, 2001).

public policy is needed throughout the Arab world that will make education a priority. Nothing less than a renaissance – drawing on the dynamism latent to Arabic, and centred on the revitalization of the language, its teaching – is required for Arabic to remain a *lingua franca* that allows Arabs to take their place confidently in the knowledge society.'[1]

Being a religious and literary medium for more than fourteen centuries, Arabic admittedly does tax its own speakers with a legacy of problems, which have occupied Arab scholars, educational institutions and academies for more than a century. Most vexing among them undoubtedly is the dichotomy between the written and spoken varieties. But there is also the lack of continuously updated dictionaries or sources incorporating current usages in Arabic. The latter would serve the needs of both native and non-native speakers and should greatly facilitate the task of translators.

While these language difficulties may limit non-native speakers' direct access to Arabic literature, they should not be viewed as an insurmountable hurdle for serious students or competent translators, nor should they be used to discourage translation from Arabic. Indeed, if a genuine and positive dialogue is to be maintained between the Arab world and the West, the translation of Arabic literature should be pursued and supported on a larger scale.

Needless to say, any literary translation has its challenges and problems, whether it involves Arabic or other languages. It requires, among other qualifications, a high degree of linguistic and cultural or spiritual competence in the original and the target languages. Samuel Hazo, the Arab–American poet and translator, who translated *Adonis* into English, suggests that, 'even the possession of such spiritual and linguistic fluency in the ideal translator is of dubious value if the translator is not of the same visionary orientation as the person he is translating' (Hazo1999: 24).[2] In some cases, a translation of a text may require numerous drafts or revisions before a satisfying version is produced. According to Eileen Kato, a translator of Japanese literature, 'she has produced up to a hundred translations of a single poem without getting something that satisfied her' (Kizuki Chiaki 2003).[3] The leading American poet and translator Robert Bly recalled that a noted Spanish speaker found no fewer

1. Mishka Moujabber Mourani, 'Arabic Teaching at Crisis Point', *Manchester Guardian Weekly* (March 18–24, 2004): 4. The author is senior vice-president of the International College in Beirut.
2. Samuel Hazo, 'On Translating Adonis and Nadia Tueni: The Many Definitions of a Translator', *aljadid* No. 26 (Winter 1999): 24.
3. Kizuki Chiaki, 'Sense and Sensibility', *Look Japan* 48.562 (January 2003): 36–38 or www.lookjapan.com (January 2003/ Culture Feature).

than twenty errors in a translation he made of a twenty-line Spanish poem, in spite of his having worked on it for months (Robert Bly 1985: 87).[1] These and many other cases related to literary translation should dispel the notion that Arabic is a uniquely troublesome or impenetrable language.

Mahfuz in American Publications

A careful reading of the bibliography will reveal the slowly but gradually increasing visibility of Mahfuz. This occurs in three phases, beginning with a marginal presence (1950–1970), proceeding to a phase of more extensive representation, though still restricted to a largely scholarly audience (1970–1987); and a third phase from 1988 when Mahfuz became the first Arab Nobel Laureate.

The first important observation that can be made about the American reception of Mahfuz is its multinational or international character, for many, if not most of the participants or mediators are Arab, European (mainly British) and other foreign-born writers. All have in varying degrees contributed to the growth of interest in Mahfuz or modern Arabic literature. However, special reference should be made to two Mahfuzian scholars, Roger Allen and Trevor LeGassick, for their pioneering and continued work, in the form of both translations and literary studies since 1963 (LeGassick) and 1970 (Allen).

The early phase (1950–1970) in particular reflects the participation of several Arab scholars who provided an overview of modern Arabic literature with occasional reference to Mahfuz. They include Abushady, Ahmed, Husayn, Khalfallah, Midani and Sfeir. To my knowledge, the earliest reference to Mahfuz was made in 1951 by Ahmad Zaki Abushady (known as Abu Shadi; 1892–1955), a major Egyptian poet who emigrated to the United States in 1946 following a long literary career in his homeland. Abushady's article 'Contemporary Egyptian Literature' was mainly concerned with the contributions of established poets, critics, novelists and other writers; it offered only a brief comment on the works of younger novelists by citing their names (Mahfuz and others) and suggesting that, in the field of fiction, 'Egypt has assumed the leadership over other Arabic-speaking countries' (95). In addition, the article alludes to the widely held belief that Taha Husayn (d.1973) was the writer most qualified to be a candidate for the Nobel Prize. Here we may recall that Arab advocacy for one or more authors as candidates for the

---

1. Robert Bly, 'The Eight Stages of Translation', in *Literary, Linguistic and Philological Perspectives*, ed. William Frawley. Newark, DE: University of Delaware Press, 1984: 67–89. A very informative essay on stages of translation.

Nobel Prize goes back as far as the late 1920s (Hall 209–210; Nijland 232). As we shall see, other passing references were made in the 1950s to Mahfuz, but more substantive accounts of his works began to appear a decade later in essays published by other Arab writers such as Akram Midani (1960) and George Sfeir (1961, 1965 and 1966).

The first American writer to cite Mahfuz for his 'excellent works' was Kermit Schoonover, who in the 1950s published several illuminating and well-balanced articles on Egypt's literature. In a paper presented to the Indiana University Conference on Oriental–Western Literary Relations (1954), Schoonover suggested that one must look to the younger writers in Egypt (whom he did not identify) 'for the continued development of the novel' and added: 'I would recommend to your attention two or three excellent books by Najib Mahfuz and venture to predict that some rather first-rate novels will be produced by this younger and more realistic set of writers' (1955: 142). As a professor affiliated with the American University in Cairo, Schoonover was undoubtedly in a position to provide more specific details about Mahfuz and his works. Regrettably, both his presentation at Indiana University and his other articles, particularly his 'Survey of the Best Modern Arabic Books' (1952), failed to shed light on Mahfuz, though they are noted for their details about other Egyptian writers. Perhaps this is due to Schoonover's focus on the earlier, more established generation of Egyptian writers and the fact that his articles were written during Mahfuz's self-imposed silence (1952–1959) and before the publication of the trilogy that earned Mahfuz the State Prize for Literature in 1956 and the prominence he has enjoyed ever since.

It was also at Indiana University, in the 1960s, that Trevor LeGassick made the earliest translations of Mahfuz's novels. LeGassick, who introduced the novelist in his courses while teaching at Indiana (1963–1966), published both his study of Mahfuz's trilogy (1963) and his translation of *Midaq Alley* (1966) in Beirut. Other translations were also published abroad by American institutions or in American-sponsored publications in Beirut or Cairo: *Middle East Forum* (American University of Beirut), American Research Center in Egypt and the American University in Cairo. These facts illustrate the circuitous route by which Mahfuz and other modern Arabic literature reached an American audience. (Ironically ignored, marginalized or neglected for many years in the US, *Midaq Alley* received a more favourable recognition in Harold Bloom's work *The Western Canon* (1994), being one of six titles Bloom had chosen from Arabic. The five others were Mahfuz's novels *Fountain and Tomb* and *Miramar*, Taha Husayn's (1889–1973) *An Egyptian Childhood*, *Selected Poems* by Adunis or Adonis (Ali Ahmad Sa'id) and Mahmud Darwish's *The Music of Human Flesh* (Bloom: 559).)

No discussion of the post-1950 period can ignore the positive impact that the newly established Middle East/Near East programmes had on the study and advancement of Arabic literature in the US. It was inevitable that such academic development and the teaching of Arabic at numerous colleges and universities would create conditions favourable for the dissemination of information on the literature or culture of the Arab world. Thus, varieties of textbooks, readers or anthologies were prepared in response to the new situation and began to contribute, albeit in a modest way, to an appreciation of Arabic literature. The bibliography lists a few examples of such works, most of which include material on Mahfuz: Abboud (1971), Bellamy (1963), Boullata (1980), Brinner and Khouri (1961/1971, 1962), Fry and King (1974), Hamalian (1978), Kritzeck (1970), LeGassick (1979) and Ziadeh (1964).

Nevertheless, it is important to note that this positive development failed, until the late 1980s, to generate a wider circulation of Mahfuz's works or Arabic literature beyond the limited confines of a small, scholarly readership. At least three types of evidence can be adduced for this assertion.

First, no major commercial press became involved in the publication of Mahfuz until 1989. It is relevant to recall Edward Said's personal experience with a major New York publisher, who declined to publish Mahfuz a few years before he was awarded the Nobel Prize, telling Said (1990) that, 'The problem is that Arabic is a controversial language'. In his well-known article 'Embargoed Literature', Said pondered the root of the culturally biased approach to the Arabs and their culture:

What, exactly, the publisher meant is still a little vague to me – but that Arabs and their language were somehow not respectable and consequently dangerous, *louche*, unapproachable, was perfectly evident to me then and, alas, now. For of all the major world literatures, Arabic remains relatively unknown and unread in the West, for reasons that are unique, even remarkable, at a time when tastes here for the non-European are more developed than ever before and, even more compelling, contemporary Arabic literature is at a particularly interesting juncture. (278)

To understand Said's disappointment with the American publishing establishment one needs only to glance at the record of Mahfuz's publishers since 1966 (when his first novel appeared in Beirut). As the first part of the bibliography indicates, no major commercial publisher embarked on publishing Mahfuz until after he was awarded the Nobel Prize. Indeed, even representatives of Mahfuz's American publisher in Cairo, the American University Press, seem to have had doubts about the wisdom of the whole enterprise of translating Mahfuz or other Egyptian writers. Writing in 1980, Christopher Wren, the Cairo Bureau Chief of *The New York Times*, noted with a measure of appreciation 'the richness of plot and language in the best Egyptian literature', but was surprised to discover that so little of it was available in English translation and that only two of Mahfuz's novels were published in English. According to Wren, the director of the American University Press referred to the novels' 'limited appeal' and wondered, 'Why should you bother to translate something that is going to be read by specialists anyway?' (Wren: 23). It should be noted, however, that the same press was accorded a central role in the awarding of the Nobel Prize to Mahfuz in 1988, as John Rodenbeck, the former director, maintains in his book *Reading Egypt: Literature, History, and Culture* (2000). According to Rodenbeck, 'the awarding … was largely due to a sixteen-year campaign by the Press [AUCP] to get the genius of Egypt's great novelist acknowledged in the West' (ix).

Second, two small presses, Three Continents Press (Washington, DC) and Bibliotheca Islamica (Minneapolis), which have been active in promoting Arabic and (in the case of the former) other third world literatures, had limited success in marketing Mahfuz's works before 1988. According to Eden Lipson (1990) and other sources, Mahfuz's novels were selling at a rate ranging from 200 to about 1,000 copies a year.

Lastly, Mahfuz's works were rarely reviewed in mainstream journals or library-oriented publications, a fact that obviously restricted their circulation.

The post-Nobel period, on the other hand, marked a turnaround in the reception of Mahfuz's works in America. Apart from the relatively greater public demand for his works and the wider audience they began to reach (as the records of some public libraries suggest), Mahfuz's works have received favourable reviews and much broader recognition since 1988. More recent anthologies of world literature such as Madden (1990) and Loughery (1994) indicate a tendency to include Mahfuz and other non-European authors.

Novelists such as Coetzee, Ghosh and Hower are among a new wave of reviewers or writers to bring Mahfuz's literary merits to a larger audience. Commenting on Mahfuz's *Palace Walk*, Hower, for instance, observes that, 'now, finally, readers can see for themselves why Mr Mahfouz has long been considered the finest Arab writer of modern times', and concludes his review with an optimistic note: 'The universal appeal of Mr Mahfouz's characters and his insight into the role of religion in their lives will go a long way toward demystifying Western readers' views of the Middle East' (11). Both Coetzee and Ghosh refer, likewise, to Mahfuz's 'solid achievement', his artistic skills and the intrinsic literary value of his works. Ghosh further states that the award 'was several decades overdue', suggesting that there are other more innovative or imaginative writers in Arabic today (32). A recent review of Loughery's *Into the Widening World* (1994) describes in positive terms 'this heartfelt anthology of brilliant voices from twenty-two countries' and characterizes Mahfuz's story as 'perhaps most charming of all' (*Publishers Weekly* November 21, 1994: 72).

The fact that Mahfuz's works are known as literary chronicles of modern Egypt has led to the proliferation of political commentaries or citations in a variety of contexts, whether in relation to Egypt, Islam, the Israel/Palestinian conflict or other issues including the Rushdie affair. There has emerged, in other words, a fascination with Mahfuz not as a novelist but as a political thinker whose views are sought or cited in support of a particular view. Indeed, even the Nobel Prize itself has been linked to Mahfuz's stand on the peace treaty between Egypt and Israel, to the point of implying a non-literary factor behind the Nobel Committee's choice. 'In Mahfuz,' writes Kessler, for example, 'the Nobel panellists found a safe bet: a humanist who called for peace with Israel and would be palatable to the Western press' (60). The fascination with Mahfuz's views does serve to introduce him and, perhaps, Arabic literature to a wider audience, but by focusing on controversial issues it may also perpetuate biased impressions about Egyptian society, the Arab world or Islam. Note, for example, Dickey's reference to 'the Islamic grudge against Mahfouz' or his claim that, 'it's not Mahfouz's views on God or Zion that most offend the righteous' but the fact that Mahfuz is known to the fundamentalists as 'sex teacher' (1989: 236, 237).

Other writers suggest that, 'in the eyes of fundamentalists Mahfouz's novels are un-Islamic' or that, 'Mahfouz has been criticized by orthodox Islamic bodies over nearly six decades' (Roberts: 186). What is disturbing about such observations is not only their inaccuracy but also their negative overtones and the distorted perception they tend to reinforce.

As has been said, the Nobel Prize awarded to Mahfuz in 1988 represents an important milestone in the history of the American reception of modern Arabic literature. As a symbolic act of recognition, it generated a wider circulation and awareness of Mahfuz as an accomplished representative of Arabic literature. It also served to vindicate what numerous scholars had been saying for decades about the high level of artistic achievement attained by contemporary Arab writers, including Mahfuz.

Bibliography

This bibliography lists items published in the United States or by American institutions abroad (mainly the American University in Cairo Press, here abbreviated to AUCP), irrespective of their authors' nationality or national origin. A few exceptional titles published elsewhere are listed because of their relevance to the issues under discussion. The bibliography is divided into two parts, before and after 1988, the year Najib Mahfuz was awarded the Nobel Prize. In the case of book reviews, only the title of the work reviewed and the source are given since the purpose of the listing is to indicate primarily the extent of American periodical coverage given to Mahfuz's works. Exceptions include detailed review articles or reviews written by novelists such Coetzee, Ghosh and Hower.

Abbreviations

BHNM Beard, Michael and Adnan Haydar, eds. *Naguib Mahfouz: From Regional Fame to Global Recognition.* Syracuse, NY: Syracuse University Press, 1993.

CPNM LeGassick, Trevor, ed. *Critical Perspectives on Naguib Mahfouz.* Washington, DC: Three Continents Press, 1991.

Part I: Pre-1988 Publications

A. Translations

1. Novels and Novellas

Autumn Quail, trans. Roger Allen. Cairo: AUCP, 1986.

The Beggar, trans. Kristin Walker Henry and Narriman Khales Al-Warraki. Cairo: AUCP, 1986.

The Beginning and the End, trans. Ramses Hanna Awad. Cairo: AUCP, 1985.

Children of Gebelawi, trans. Philip Stewart. Washington, DC: Three Continents Press, 1981.

Midaq Alley, trans. Trevor LeGassick. Beirut: Khayats, 1966; Washington, DC: Three Continents Press, 1977, 1981.

Miramar, trans. Fatma Moussa-Mahmoud. London: Heinemann, 1978. (See other US editions under Since 1988 below).

Mirrors, trans. Roger Allen. Minneapolis: Bibliotheca Islamica, 1977.

Respected Sir, trans. Rasheed El-Enany. Cairo: AUCP, 1987.

The Search, trans. Mohamed Islam, ed. Magdi Wahba. Cairo: AUCP, 1987.

The Thief and the Dogs, trans. Trevor LeGassick and M. M. Badawi. Cairo: AUCP, 1984. See also Elyas below under Studies.

Wedding Song, trans. Olive E. Kenny. Cairo: AUCP, 1984.

2. Short Stories and Excerpts

'An Alarming Voice', trans. A. F. Cassis. *Literature East and West* 13 (1969): 386–394.

'Alleyways' [An excerpt from *Fountain and Tomb*], trans. Soad Sobhi et al. *Michigan Quarterly Review* 23 (1984): 503–509.

'The Chase', trans. Roger Allen. *Mundus Artium* 10.1 (1977): 134–162.

'Child of Ordeal', trans. Akef Abadir and Roger Allen. *Arab World* August–September 1971: 10–18.

'Child of Suffering', trans. Menahem Milson and Ruth Kuselewitz. *International Journal of Middle East Studies* 3 (1972): 326–338.

'Child's Paradise', trans. Akef Abadir and Roger Allen. *Arab World* September–October 1970: 14–16.

'The Conjurer Made off with the Dish', trans. Denys Johnson-Davies in his *Egyptian Short Stories*. Washington, DC: Three Continents Press, 1978: 61–67. Reprinted in *The Art of the Tale: An International Anthology of Short Stories 1945–1985*, ed. Daniel Halpern. New York: Viking Penguin, 1986: 411–416. See also Loughery 1994.

'The Fashioner of Sick Men'. [From *Midaq Alley*] Trans. James R. King. In *An Anthology of Middle Eastern Literature from the Twentieth Century*, eds C. George Fry and James R. King. Springfield, OH: 1974: 110–113.

'Filfil', trans. F. el-Manssour. *Middle East Forum* June 1961: 38–39.

'Five Tales from Alleyways'. [An excerpt from *Fountain and Tomb*] Trans. James Kenneson with Soad Sobhi and Essam Fatouh. *Ploughshares* 11.4 (1985): 191–196.

God's World, trans. Akef Abadir and Roger Allen. Minneapolis: Bibliotheca Islamica, 1973. [includes 'God's World', 'The Happy Man', 'A Photograph', 'An Extraordinary Official', 'The Whisper of Madness', 'Child's Paradise', 'Shahrazad', 'The Drug Addict and the Bomb', 'The Singing Drunkard', 'The Barman', 'A Dream', 'Passers-By', 'The Black Cat Tavern', 'Under the Bus Shelter', 'Sleep', 'The Heart Doctor's Ghost', 'The Window on the Thirty-fifth Floor', 'The Prisoner of War's Uniform', 'An Unnerving Sound' and 'The Wilderness']

'Hanzal and the Policemen', trans. Azza Kararah, revised by David Kirkhaus. *Arabic Writing Today: The Short Story*, ed. Mahmud Manzalaoui. Cairo: American Research Center in Egypt, 1968: 129–136.

'Investigation', trans. Roger Allen. *Edebiyat* 3.1 (1978): 27–24.

'The Legacy', trans. Akef Abadir and Roger Allen. *Arab World* November–December 1970: 11–20.

'The Mosque in the Alley', trans. with notes by Joseph P. O'Kane. *Muslim World* 63 (1973): 28–38.

'The Mosque in the Narrow Lane', trans. Nadia Farag, revised by Josephine Wahba. *Arabic Writing Today: The Short Story*, ed. Mahmud Manzalaoui. Cairo: American Research Center in Egypt, 1968: 117–128.

'Traveler with Hand Luggage', trans. Denys Johnson-Davies. *Under the Naked Sky: Short Stories from the Arab World* Cairo: AUCP, 2000: 23–26.

'An Old Photograph', trans. Roger Allen. *Nimrod* 24: 2 (1981): 51–55. Reprinted in *Perceptions of Aging in Literature: A Cross-Cultural Study*, eds Prisca von Dorotka Bagnell and Patricia Spencer Soper. New York: Greenwood Press, 1989: 118–126.

'The Pasha's Daughter', trans. F. el-Manssour. *Middle East Forum* October 1960: 38–42.

'Tales from Alleyways', trans. Soad Sobhi et al. [An excerpt from *Fountain and Tomb*] *The Missouri Review* 8.2 (1985): 88–95. Reprinted in *The Best of the Missouri Review: Fiction 1978–1990*, eds Speer I. Morgan et al. Columbia: University of Missouri Press, 1991: 252–260.

'The Tavern of the Black Cat', trans. A. F. Cassis. *Contemporary Literature in Translation* 19 (1974): 5–8.

'Three Tales', trans. Soad Sobhy and Jim Kenneson [An excerpt from *Fountain and Tomb*] *Antaeus* Winter/Spring 1981: 139–144.

'Zaabalawi', trans. Denys Johnson-Davies. In *Modern Arab Short Stories* London: Oxford University Press, 1967: 137–147. Reprinted in *Modern Islamic Literature*, ed. James Kritzeck. New York: Holt, Rinehart & Winston, 1970. 226–235. See also Mack, Maynard 1992.

B. Book Reviews

Autumn Quail. World Literature Today 61 (1987): 148.

Children of Gebelawi. Middle East Journal 36 (1982): 255–256. *Teachers College Record* 84 (1983): 773–776. *World Literature Today* 56 (1982): 398.

God's World. Books Abroad (now *World Literature Today*) 48 (1974): 617. *Choice* April 12, 1975: 230.

Midaq Alley. Catholic Library World September 1980: 81.

Miramar. Middle East Journal 34 (1980): 500–501. *World Literature Today* 53 (1979): 739–740.

Mirrors. World Literature Today 52 (1978): 686.

The Thief and the Dogs. World Literature Today 60 (1986): 684.

C. Selected Studies, Interviews and Related Items

Abadir, Akef and Roger Allen, 'Nagib Mahfuz, His World of Literature', *Arab World* September–October 1970: 7–14; November–December 1970: 9–10; and August–September 1971: 7–9.

Abboud, Peter et al., eds, *Modern Standard Arabic: Intermediate Level* Part II. Ann Arbor: University of Michigan, Center for Near Eastern and North African Studies, 1971: 469–487 [Excerpts in Arabic from Mahfuz's *Mirrors*].

Abushady, A. Z., 'Contemporary Egyptian Literature', *Middle Eastern Affairs* 2 (1951): 90–97.

Accad, Evelyne, 'Veil of Shame: The Role of Women in the Contemporary Fiction of North Africa and the Arab World', Dissertation for Indiana University, 1974. Published as a book under the same title. Sherbrooke, Quebec: Naaman, 1978: 128–133.

—— 'The Prostitute in Arab and North African Fiction', *The Image of the Prostitute in Modern Literature*, ed. Pierre L. Horn and Mary Beth Pringle. New York: Ungar 1984: 63–75.

Allen, Roger, *The Arabic Novel: An Historical and Critical Introduction* Syracuse, NY: Syracuse University Press, 1982: especially 55–62, 101–107.

—— 'Aspects of Technique in the Modern Arabic Short Story', *World Literature Today* 60 (1986): 199–206.

—— 'Egyptian Literature', *African Literature in the 20th Century: A Guide* Based on the *Encyclopedia of World Literature in the 20th Century*, revised edition, ed. Leonard S. Klein. New York: Ungar, 1986: 39–46.

—— 'Mahfuz Naguib', *World Authors: 1975–1980*, ed. Vineta Colby. New York: Wilson, 1985: 478–482.

—— 'Mahfuz's *Mirrors*', *American Research Center in Egypt Newsletter* October 1971: 9–14.

—— '*Mirrors* by Najib Mahfuz', *Muslim World* 62 (1972): 115–125; 63 (1973): 15–27. Reprinted in *CPNM*: 131–150.

—— 'Najib Mahfuz', *Encyclopedia of World Literature in the Twentieth Century*, ed. Leonard Klein. New York: 1981, Vol. 3: 178–179. Reprinted in *African*

Literatures in the 20th Century: A Guide Based on the *Encyclopedia of World Literature in the 20th Century*, revised edition. New York: Ungar, 1986: 54–56.

—— 'Some Recent Works of Najib Mahfuz: A Critical Analysis', *Journal of the American Research Center in Egypt* 14 (1977): 101–110.

—— See Abadir, Akef.

Altoma, Salih J. 'Socio-Political Themes in the Contemporary Arabic Novel: 1950–1970', *The Cry of Home: Cultural Nationalism and the Modern Writer*, ed. H. E. Lewlad. Knoxville: University of Tennessee Press, 1972: 351–373, especially 352–356.

—— 'Westernization and Islam in Modern Arabic Fiction', *Yearbook of Comparative and General Literature* 20 (1971): 81–88, especially 84–85.

—— 'al-Talaqqi al-amriki li'l-adab al-'arabi' [The American Reception of Arabic Literature], *al-Istishraq* [Orientalism], ed. M. J. Musawi. Vol. II. Baghdad: Cultural Affairs, 1987: 71–76.

Alwan, Mohammed Bakir, 'A Bibliography of Modern Arabic Fiction in English Translation', *Middle East Journal* 26 (1972): 195–200.

Amyuni, Mona T., 'Images of Arab Women in *Midaq Alley* by Naguib Mahfouz, and *Season of Migration to the North* by Tayeb Salih', *International Journal of Middle East Studies* 17 (1985): 25–36.

Awad, Louis, 'Cultural and Intellectual Developments in Egypt since 1952', *Egypt since the Revolution*, ed. P. J. Vatikiotis. New York and London: Praeger/Allen and Unwin, 1968: 143–161.

Badawi, M. M., 'Commitment in Contemporary Arabic Literature', *Journal of World History* 14 (1972): 858–879. Reprinted in *Critical Perspectives on Modern Arabic Literature*. See Boullata below: 23–44.

Barakat, Halim, *Visions of Social Reality in the Contemporary Arab Novel* Washington, DC: Georgetown University, Center for Contemporary Arab Studies, 1977: especially 12–21.

Bellamy, James A. et al., eds, *Contemporary Arabic Readers IV. Short Stories*. Ann Arbor: University of Michigan Press, 1963.

Berque, Jacques, *Cultural Expression in Arab Society Today*, trans. Robert W. Stookey. Austin: University of Texas Press, 1978: especially 57, 215, 225–226, 229–231.

Boullata, Issa, ed. *Critical Perspectives on Modern Arabic Literature* Washington, DC: Three Continents Press, 1980 [includes: LeGassick's 'Najib Mahfouz Trilogy', pp. 61–67; 'A Malaise in Cairo', pp. 68–81; Mikhail's 'Broken Idols', pp. 83–93; and Hafez's 'The Egyptian Novel in the Sixties', pp. 171–187].

Brinner, William M. and Mounah A. Khouri, *Advanced Arabic Readers I: Selections from the Modern Novel and Short Story* Berkeley: University of California Press, 1961 [Mahfuz is not represented in this edition]. Published under the title *Readings in Modern Arabic Literature. Part One: The Short Story and the Novel* Leiden: Brill, 1971 [Includes a selection by Mahfuz, see 30–46, 221–253].

—— *Advanced Arabic Readers II: Expository Writing: Intellectual and Social Trends* Berkeley: University of California Press, 1962.

el-Calamawy, Sahair, 'The Impact of Tradition on the Development of Modern Arabic Literature', *Arab and American Cultures*, ed. George N. Atiyeh. Washington, DC: American Enterprise Institute for Public Policy Research, 1979: 47–53.

Cargas, Harry James, 'Modern Arabic Literature: A Beginning', *Catholic Library World* 52 (1980–81): 81–82.

Colby, Vineta, ed., *World Authors: 1975-1980* New York: Wilson, 1985: 478–482.

Cooke, Miriam, *The Anatomy of an Egyptian Intellectual: Yahya Haqqi* Washington, DC: Three Continents Press, 1984: 11, 63, 67–68, 84, 90, 138 [Mainly on Haqqi's views of Mahfuz].

Cowan, David, 'Literary Trends in Egypt since 1952', *Egypt since the Revolution*, ed. P. J. Vatikiotis. New York and London: Praeger/Allen and Unwin, 1968: 162–177, especially 172–174.

Deeb, Marius, 'Najib Mahfuz's *Midaq Alley*: A Socio-Cultural Analysis', *British Society for Middle Eastern Studies Bulletin* 10 (1983): 121–130. Reprinted in *CPNM*: 27–36.

Elyas, Adel Ata, 'A Thief in Search of his Identity: Naguib Mahfouz's *Al-Liss Wa'l-kilab (The Thief and the Dogs)*: A Critical Analysis with a Translation of the Novel', Dissertation for Oklahoma State University, 1979. Published as a book. Jeddah: Dar Al-Shorouq, 1987.

Frenz, Horst and G. L. Anderson, eds, *Indiana University Conference on Oriental–Western Literary Relations* Chapel Hill: University of North Carolina Press, 1955.

Fowles, John, 'Introduction', Mahfuz's *Miramar*, trans. Fatma Moussa-Mahmud. London: Heinemann, 1978: vii-xv. See also US editions.

Fry, George C. and James R. King, *An Anthology of Middle Eastern Literature from the Twentieth Century* Springfield, OH: 1974: 110–113 [Mahfuz's 'The Fashioner of Sick Men'].

Gibb, H. A. R., 'Studies in Contemporary Arabic Literature', in *Studies on the Civilization of Islam*, eds Stanford J. Shaw and William R. Polk. Boston: Beacon Press, 1962: 245–319.

Gordon, Haim, 'Naguib Mahfouz: The Search for an Egyptian Thou', *Dance, Dialogue, and Despair: Existentialist Philosophy and Education for Peace in Israel* Tuscaloosa: University of Alabama Press, 1986: 151–173.

Hafez, Sabry, 'The Egyptian Novel in the Sixties', *Journal of Arabic Literature* 7 (1976): 68–84. Reprinted in Boullata's *Critical Perspectives on Modern Arabic Literature*: 171–187.

Hall, Trowbridge, 'Egypt's Literature', In his *Egypt in Silhouette* New York: Macmillan, 1928: 208–288, especially 208–212.

Halpern, Daniel, ed., *The Art of the Tale: An International Anthology of Short Stories 1945–1985* New York: Viking, 1986: 411–416.

Hamalian, Leo and John D. Yohannan, eds, *New Writing from the Middle East* A Mentor Book. New York: New American Library, 1978.

Haywood, John A., *Modern Arabic Literature 1800–1970* New York: St Martin's Press, 1972: especially 206–207.

Heikal, Mohamed, *Autumn of Fury: The Assassination of Sadat* New York: Random House, 1983: especially 47–49.

Hitti, Philip K., 'Arab Literary Contributions to Western Thought and Culture', *World Literatures*, eds Joseph Remenyi et al. Pittsburgh: University of Pittsburgh Press, 1956: 15–25.

Husayn, Taha, 'The Modern Renaissance of Arabic Literature', *Books Abroad* (now *World Literature Today*) 29 (1955): 5–18.

Hutchins, William, 'Naguib Mahfouz', *Contemporary Foreign Language Writers*, eds James Vinson and Daniel Kirkpatrick. New York: St Martin's Press, 1984: 228–230.

Jurji, Edward J., 'Arabic Literature', *Encyclopedia of Literature*, ed. Joseph T. Shipley. New York: 1946. Vol 1: 19–48, especially 39–46 covering modern period.

Kedourie, Elie, 'Critics in Despair: *The Return of Consciousness* by Tawfiq al-Hakim and *An Unfinished Odyssey* by Cecil Hourani', *The New Republic* March 24, 1986: 32–36, especially 33.

Khalfallah, Muhammad, 'Literary Life in Modern Egypt in its Relation to the Contemporary World', *Muslim World* 44 (1954): 85–100.

Khouri, Mounah, 'Literature', *The Genius of Arab Civilization: Source of Renaissance*, ed. John S. Badeau et al. New York: New York University Press, 1975: 17–45, especially 43.

Kritzeck, James, ed., *Modern Islamic Literature* New York: Holt, Rinehart & Winston, 1970: 226–235 [Mahfuz's 'Zaabalawi'].

LeGassick, Trevor, 'Arab Prose and Poetry, A Prod and Reflection on Unity and Progress', *Mid-East* October 1969: 7–13.

—— 'The Literature of Modern Egypt', *Books Abroad* 46 (1972): 232–237, especially 236–237.

—— 'Mahfuz's *al-Karnak*. The Quiet Conscience of Nasir's Egypt Revealed', *Middle East Journal* 31 (1977): 205–212. Reprinted in *CPNM*: 151–162.

—— 'A Malaise in Cairo: Three Contemporary Egyptian Authors', *Middle East Journal* 21 (1967): 145–156.

—— 'Najib Mahfouz Trilogy', *Middle East Forum* February 1963: 31–34.

—— ed., *Major Themes in Modern Arabic Thought: An Anthology* Ann Arbor: University of Michigan Press, 1979.

Leuchtenburg, William E., 'The American Perception of the Arab World', *Arab and American Cultures*, ed. George N. Atiyeh. Washington, DC: American Enterprise Institute for Public Policy Research, 1979: 15–25.

Magill, Frank N. *Critical Survey of Long Fiction: Foreign Language Series*. 5 vols. Englewood Cliffs, NJ: Salem Press, 1984.

—— *Critical Survey of Poetry: Foreign Language Series*. 5 vols. Englewood Cliffs, NJ: Salem Press, 1984.

Mahfuz, Najib, 'Mahfuz, Naguib', trans. Roger Allen. *World Authors 1975–1980*, ed. Vineta Colby. New York: Wilson, 1985: 478–479.

Mahmoud, Mohamed, 'The Unchanging Hero in a Changing World: Najib Mahfuz's al-Liss wa'l-Kilab', *Journal of Arabic Literature* 15 (1984): 58–75. Reprinted *CPNM*: 115–130.

Massoud, Mary, 'Christianity in the Literary Works of Muslim Egyptian Writers', *Studies in the Humanities* 13 (1986): 11–115.

Midani, Akram, 'New Forms in Arabic Literature and Drama', *The Arab World* November 1960: 12–13.

Mikhail, Mona, 'Broken Idols: The Death of Religion as Reflected in Two Short Stories by Idris and Mahfuz', *Journal of Arabic Literature* 5 (1974): 147–157. Reprinted in Boullata's *Critical Perspectives on Modern Arabic Literature*: 83–94.

—— *Images of Arab Women: Fact and Fiction* Washington, DC: Three Continents Press, 1979: especially 102–107.

Milson, Menahim, 'An Allegory on the Social and Cultural Crisis in Egypt: 'Walid al-'ana' by Najib Mahfuz', *International Journal of Middle East Studies* 3 (1972): 324–347.

—— 'Some Aspects of the Modern Egyptian Novel', *Muslim World* 60 (1970): 237–246.

Moosa, Matti I., 'The Growth of Modern Arabic Fiction', *Critique: Studies in Modern Fiction* 11 (1968): 5–19, especially 16–18.

—— *The Origins of Modern Arabic Fiction* Washington, DC: Three Continents Press, 1983: especially 179–181.

Nijland, C., 'A Congress of Arabic Language and Literature in Cairo, May 1927', *Proceedings of the Ninth Congress of the Union Européenne des Arabisants et Islamisants*, ed. Rudolph Peters. Leiden: Brill, 1981: 230–240.

Peled, M., *Religion, My Own: The Literary Works of Najib Mahfuz*. New Brunswick: Transaction Books, 1983.

Polk, William R., ed., *Perspective of the Arab World: An Atlantic Supplement. The Atlantic* October 1956: especially 124 (the editor's introduction) and 161–164 (Ahmed's article 'The Present Mood in Literature') [A pioneering attempt devoted mainly to modern Arabic literature, the supplement includes selections representing several noted novelists but Mahfuz is not among them].

Poss, Stanley, 'Notes on Modern Egyptian Short Stories', *Critique: Studies in Modern Fiction* 11 (1968): 20–24.

Reid, Donald M., 'The 'Sleeping Philosopher' of Nagib Mahfuz's *Mirrors*', *The Muslim World* 74 (1984): 1–11.

Ronnow, Gretchen, 'The Oral vs. the Written: A Dialectic of Worldviews in Najib Mahfouz's *Children of Our Alley*', *Al-'Arabiyya* 17 (1984): 87–118.

Said, Edward W., *Orientalism* New York: Pantheon, 1978.

—— 'Introduction', *Days of Dust* by Halim Barakat, trans. Trevor LeGassick. Wilmette: The Medina University Press International, 1974: ix–xxxiv.

Sakkut, Hamdi, *The Egyptian Novel: 1913–1952*. Cairo: American University in Cairo, 1970: especially 114–142.

Samaan, Angele B., 'Nationalist Themes and the Developing Form of the Egyptian Novel', *Studies in the Humanities* 13 (1986): 11–20, especially 17–19.

Schoonover, Kermit, 'Contemporary Egyptian Authors', *Muslim World* 45 (1955): 26–36, 359–370; and 47 (1957): 36–45 [Four authors are covered:

Tawfiq Al-Hakim and Abbas Mahmud al-Aqqad in part I; Taha Husayn in part II; and Mahmud Taymur and the Short Story in part III].

—— 'Modern Arabic Literature', *Indiana University Conference on Oriental–Western Literary Relations*, eds Horst Frenz and G. L. Anderson. Chapel Hill, NC: University of North Carolina Press, 1955: 137–147.

—— 'Some Observations on Modern Arabic Literature', *Muslim World* 44 (1954): 20–30.

—— 'A Survey of the Best Modern Arabic Books', *Muslim World* 42 (1952): 48–55.

Seymour-Smith, Martin, 'Arabic Literature', *The Guide to Modern World Literature* New York: Peter Bedrick Books, 1985: 180–183.

Sfeir, George, 'The Contemporary Arabic Novel', *Daedalus* 95 (1966): 941–960. Reprinted in *Fiction in Several Languages*, ed. Henry Pyre. Boston: Houghton Mifflin, 1968: 60–79 especially 66–72.

—— 'Writer with a Universal View', *The Arab World* February 1965: 5–6.

—— 'Writing in Arabic', *NYT Book Review* September 23, 1962: 48–49.

El-Shamy, Hasan, 'The Traditional Structure of Sentiments in Mahfouz's Trilogy: A Behavioristic Text Analysis', *Al-'Arabiyya* 9 (1976): 53–74. Reprinted in *CPNM*: 51–70.

el-Sheikh, Ibrahim, 'Egyptian Women as Portrayed in the Social Novels of Najib Mahfuz', *Al-'Arabiyya* 15 (1982): 131–145. Reprinted in *CPNM*: 85–99.

Siddiq, Muhammad, 'The Contemporary Arabic Novel in Perspective', *World Literature Today* 60 (1986): 206–211.

Somekh, S., '*A Minute to Midnight*: War and Peace in the Novels of Najib Mahfouz', *Middle East Review* 20 (Winter 1987/88): 7–13.

—— 'The Sad Millenarian: An Examination of *Awlad Haratina*', *Middle Eastern Studies* 7 (1971): 49–61. Reprinted in *CPNM*: 101–114.

Vatikiotis, P. J., *The Modern History of Egypt* New York: Praeger, 1969: especially 435–437.

Vinson, James and Daniel Kilpatrick, eds, *Great Foreign Language Writers* New York: St Martin's Press, 1984.

Wakeman, John, ed., *World Authors: 1970–1975* New York: Wilson, 1980.

Wessler, A., 'Nagib Mahfuz and Secular Man', *Humaniora Islamica* 3 (1974): 105–119.

Wickens, G. M., 'Arabic Literature', *Literatures of the East*, ed. Eric B. Ceadel. London: Murray, 1953. US edition New York: Grove Press, 1959: 22–49, especially 43.

Wilbur, Donald N., ed., *United Arab Republic–Egypt* New Haven, CT: Human Relations Area Files, 1969: especially 125–126.

Winder, R. Bayly, 'Four Decades of Middle Eastern Study', *Middle East Journal* 41 (1987): 40–63.

Wren, Christopher, 'Literary Letter from Cairo: On Al-Ahram's Sixth Floor', *NYT Book Review* March 16, 1980: 3, 22.

Young, George, *Egypt* London: E. Benn, 1927: especially 284–285.

Ziadeh, Farhat J., *A Reader in Modern Literary Arabic* Princeton, NJ: Princeton University Press, 1964.

Part II: Since 1988

A. Translations

1. Novels, Novellas and Similar Works

Adrift on the Nile, trans. Jean Liardet. Cairo: AUCP, 1993; New York: Anchor Books, 1993 and Doubleday, 1993.

Akhenaten, Dweller in Truth, trans. Tagreid Abu Hassabo. Cairo: AUCP, 1998; New York: Anchor Books, 2000.

Arabian Nights and Days, trans. Denys Johnson-Davies. New York: Doubleday, 1995.

Autumn Quail New York: Doubleday, 1990.

The Beggar, trans. Kristin Walker Henry and Nariman Khales Naili al-Warraki. Cairo: AUCP, 1986, 1989; New York: Doubleday, 1990; New York: Anchor Books, 2000.

The Beginning and the End New York: Anchor Books, 1989 and Doubleday, 1989.

Children of Gebelawi Washington, DC: Three Continents Press, 1988. Revised edition 1990. Revised and augmented edition Colorado Springs: Three Continents Press, 1995; Pueblo, CO: Passeggiata Press, 1996.

Children of the Alley, trans. Peter Theroux. New York: Doubleday, 1996.

The Day the Leader Was Killed, trans. Malak Hashem. Cairo: GEBO, 1989; Cairo: AUCP, 1997; New York: Anchor Books, 2000.

Echoes of an Autobiography, trans. Denys Johnson-Davies. Foreword by Nadine Gordimer. Cairo: AUCP, 1996; New York: Doubleday, 1997, 1998.

Fountain and Tomb, trans. Soad Sobhi, Essam Fattouh and James Kennesson. Washington, DC: Three Continents Press, 1988; Colorado Springs, CO: Three Continents Press, 1994.

The Harafish, trans. Catherine Cobham. New York: Doubleday, 1993.

The Journey of Ibn Fattouma, trans. Denys Johnson-Davies. New York: Doubleday, 1992 and Anchor Books, 1993.

Khufu's Wisdom, trans. Raymond Stock. Cairo: AUCP, 2003.

Midaq Alley. Second US edition. Washington, DC: Three Continents Press, 1989; New York: Doubleday, 1992.

Midaq Alley, The Thief and the Dogs, Miramar New York: Quality Paperback Book Club, 1989.

Miramar. Second US edition. Washington, DC: Three Continents Press, 1990. First Anchor Books edition New York: Anchor Books, 1993.

Mirrors, trans. Roger Allen. Minneapolis, MN: Bibliotheca Islamica, 1990; Cairo: AUCP, 1999.

Palace of Desire, trans. William M. Hutchins, Lorne M. Kenny and Olive E. Kenny. Cairo: AUCP, 1991; New York: Doubleday, 1991.

Palace Walk, trans. William M. Hutchins and Olive E. Kenny. Cairo: AUCP, 1989; New York: Doubleday, 1990. See also *The Cairo Trilogy* New York: Alfred A. Knopf, 2001.

Rhadopis of Nubia, trans. Anthony Stock. Cairo: AUCP, 2003.

Respected Sir, trans. Rashid Enany. New York: Doubleday, 1990.

Respected Sir, The Search, Wedding Song New York: Anchor Books, 2001.

The Search. First Anchor Books edition. New York: Anchor Books, 1991. (See also *Respected Sir* 2001.)

Sugar Street, trans. William W. Hutchins and Angele Botros Samaan. Cairo: AUCP, 1992; New York: Doubleday, 1992 and Anchor Books, 1993.

Thebes at War, trans. Humphrey Davies. Cairo: AUCP, 2003.

The Thief and the Dogs New York: Doubleday, 1991.

Wedding Song. First Doubleday edition. New York: Doubleday, 1989. (See also *Respected Sir* 2001.)

See also *Naguib Mahfouz at Sidi Gaber: Reflections of a Nobel Laureate, 1994–2001* Cairo: AUCP, 2001.

2. Short Stories

Arabian Nights and Days, trans. Denys Johnson-Davies. New York: Doubleday, 1995.

Egyptian Time Short story by Mahfuz, trans. Peter Theroux. Photographs by Robert Lyons. New York: Doubleday, 1992.

'False Dawn', trans. Trevor LeGassick. *The World and I* February 1992: 433–449.

God's World Minneapolis, MN: Bibliotheca Islamica, 1988.

'The Land of Mashriq' [An excerpt from *The Journey of Ibn Fattouma*, trans. Denys Johnson-Davies. *Paris Review* Summer 1992: 43–49.]

'An Old Photograph', see the same title in the Pre-1988 section.

'Tales from Alleyways', see the same title in the Pre-1988 section.

The Time and the Place and Other Stories, trans. Denys Johnson-Davies. Cairo: AUCP, 1991; New York: Doubleday, 1991 [includes 'Zaabalawi', 'The Conjuror Made of with the Dish', 'The Answer Is No', 'The Time and The Place', 'Blessed Night', 'The Ditch', 'Half a Day', 'The Tavern of the Black Cat', 'The Lawsuit', 'The Empty Cafe', 'A Day for Saying Goodbye', 'By a Person Unknown', 'The Man and the Other Man', 'The Wasteland', 'The Norwegian Rat', 'His Majesty', 'Fear', 'At the Bus Stop', 'A Fugitive from Justice' and 'A Long-Term Plan'].

'A Visit', trans. Ismail I. Nawwab. *ARAMCO* 24: 2 (March–April 1989): 20–26.

Voices from the Other World, trans. Raymond Stock. Cairo: AUCP, 2002.

'The Whisper of Madness', trans. Roger Allen. *The World of Fiction*, ed. David Madden. Fort Worth, TX: Holt, Rinehart & Winston, 1990: 645–649.

'Zaabalawi', trans. Denys Johnson-Davies. *The Norton Anthology of World Masterpieces*, ed. Maynard Mack. Vol.2. New York: W. W. Norton, 1992: 1965–1973.

B. Book Reviews

Adrift on the Nile. *Booklist* 1 January 1993: 771; *Kirkus Reviews* 1 December 1992: 1461; *Library Journal* February 15, 1993: 193; *Publishers Weekly* December 14, 1992: 39; *New York Review of Books* November 30, 2000: 42–.

Akhenaten. *Booklist* March 15, 2000:1328; *New York Review of Books* November 30, 2000: 42–

Arabian Nights and Days. Booklist October 15, 1994: 372; *Christian Science Monitor*
26 January 1995: B 1; *Hudson Review* 48.2 (Summer 1995): 325–332; *Kirkus
Reviews* November 1, 1994: 1434–1435; *Library Journal* November 15, 1994:
87; *Publishers Weekly* October 31, 1994: 43.

Autumn Quail. Publishers Weekly July 13, 1990: 50.

The Beggar. Library Journal October 1, 1989: 119; *Middle East Journal* 42 (1988):
481; *Publishers Weekly* July 13, 1990: 49; *World Literature Today* 62 (1988):
173.

The Beginning and the End. Booklist October 1, 1989: 262; *Commentary* June 1991:
34; *Library Journal* October 1, 1989: 119; *Middle East Journal* 42 (1988): 421;
The New Republic May 7, 1990: 32; *New York Times Book Review* December
10, 1989: 9; *People* October 30, 1989: 22; *Publishers Weekly* August 25, 1989:
57; *The Review of Contemporary Fiction* 10.2 (1990): 266–267; *World Literature
Today* 62 (1988): 504.

Cairo Trilogy. Library Journal November 15, 2001; *New York Times* September 16,
2002: E1; *New York Review of Books* November 20, 2003: 32.

Children of the Alley. New York Times Book Review February 18, 1996: 26,
December 1, 1996: 35, December 8, 1996: 100; *Library Journal* December
1, 1995: 156; *Wall Street Journal* January 22, 1996: A10.

Children of Gebelawi. Connoisseur April 1989: 50; *The Washington Report on Middle
Eastern Affairs* October 1989: 47.

Echoes of an Autobiography. Booklist November 15, 1996: 547; *Library Journal*
March 1, 1997: 76; *Publishers Weekly* November 11, 1996: 66.

Fountain and the Tomb. Christian Science Monitor January 5, 1989: 11; *Connoisseur*
April 1989: 57; *International Journal of Middle East Studies* 22 (1990): 368–369;
Middle East Journal 43 (1989): 507–511; *World Literature Today* 63 (1989):
361.

The Harafish. Kirkus Reviews February 15, 1994: 167; *Library Journal* April 15,
1994: 113; *New York Review of Books* September 22, 1994: 30–33; *Publishers
Weekly* March 7, 1994: 54; *World Literature Today* 68 (1994): 874.

Khufu's Wisdom New York Review of Books November 20, 2003: 32.

The Journey of Ibn Fattouma. Choice January 1993: 803; *Kirkus Reviews* July 1, 1992;
Library Journal September 15, 1992: 94; *Publishers Weekly* July 20, 1992: 228;
World Literature Today 67 (1993): 887.

Midaq Alley. Connoisseur April 1989: 50; *Library Journal* December 1991: 198; *The
New Republic* May 7, 1990: 32; *Publishers Weekly* December 6, 1991: 66; *The
Washington Report on Middle East Affairs* January 1989: 24.

Miramar. Connoisseur April 1989: 50.

Mirrors. Washington Report on Middle East Affairs June 1990: 56–57.

Naguib Mahfouz at Sidi Gaber. Library Journal June 1, 2002; *New York Review of Books* 52 April 2002: 29.

Palace of Desire. Commentary June 1991: 34; *Commonweal* June 14, 1991: 410–411; *The Hudson Review* 44.3 (1991): 491–493; *Library Journal* January 1991: 154; *New York Times Book Review* January 20, 1991: 15; *Publishers Weekly* November 2, 1990: 63; *World Literature Today* 65 (1991): 759.

Palace Walk. The Hudson Review 44.3 (1991): 491–493; *Insight* March 5, 1990: 63; *Library Journal* December 1989: 172; *Muslim World* 80 (1990): 286–287; *National Review* February 19, 1990: 51–52; *The New Republic* May 7, 1990: 32; *Newsweek* February 26, 1990: 64; *New York Times,* January 29, 1990: 67; *New York Times Book Review* February 4, 1990: 11; *Publishers Weekly* November 3, 1989: 82.

Respected Sir. New York Times Book Review January 31, 1988: 29; *Publishers Weekly* July 13, 1990: 49.

Rhadophis of Nubia. New York Review of Books November 20, 2003: 32.

The Search. Library Journal May 15, 1991: 109; *Middle East Journal* 43 (1989): 507–511; *New York Times Book Review* August 4, 1991: 24; *Publishers Weekly* May 24,1991: 55; *Vogue* July 1991: 85; *World Literature Today* 62 (1988): 328–329.

Sugar Street. Kirkus Reviews October 15, 1991; *New York Times Book Review* March 22, 1992: 17; *Publishers Weekly* October 25, 1991: 44; *Texas Review* (Fall 1997): 83–95.

The Thief and the Dogs. Booklist October 1, 1989: 262; *Commentary* June 1991: 34; *Library Journal* October 1, 1989: 119; *The New Republic* May 7, 1990: 32; *New York Times Book Review* December 10, 1989: 5; *People* October 30, 1989: 22; *Publishers Weekly* September 8, 1989: 63; *The Review of Contemporary Fiction* 10.2 (1990): 266–267; *World Literature Today* 60 (1986): 684.

The Time and the Place and Other Stories. Kirkus Reviews April 15, 1991: 494; *Library Journal* May 15, 1991: 109; *Publishers Weekly* May 24, 1991: 44; *Vogue* July 1991: 85; *World Literature Today* 67 (1993): 226.

Wedding Song. Booklist October 1, 1989: 262; *Library Journal* October 1, 1989: 119; *The New Republic* May 7, 1990: 32; *New York Times Book Review* December 10, 1989: 9; *People Weekly* October 30, 1989: 22; *Publishers Weekly* September 8, 1989: 62; *The Review of Contemporary Fiction* 10.2 (1990): 266–267.

C. Studies, Interviews and Related Items

Abdel-Jaouad, Hedi, 'Paul Bowles à Tanger', *CELFAN Review* 7.3 (May 1988): 15–18.

Abou-Saif, Laila, 'Naguib Mahfouz: Novelist, Nobel Prize for Literature, 1988' [Interview], in her *Middle East Journal: A Woman's Journey into the Heart of the Arab World*. New York: Charles Scribner's Sons, 1990: 102–114.

Abu Ahmed, Hamed, 'From an Interview with the 1988 Nobel Prize Winner in Literature', *World Press Review* January 1989: 61.

'Against Cultural Terrorism', *New Perspectives Quarterly* Spring 1994: 34 [A brief excerpt of a declaration signed by Mahfuz and others in defence of freedom of expression].

Alcalay, Ammiel, *After Jews and Arabs*. Minneapolis, MN: University of Minnesota Press, 1993.

Allen, Roger, 'Arabic Literature and the Nobel Prize', *World Literature Today* 62 (1988): 201–203.

—— 'Najib Mahfuz: Nobel Laureate in Literature, 1988', *World Literature Today* 63 (1989): 5–9.rpt. *Twayne Companion to Contemporary World Literature*, ed. and Intro. Pamela Genova. New York: Twayne; Thomson Gale, 2003: 177–182.

—— 'Najib Mahfuz 1988', *Nobel Laureates in Literature: A Biographical Dictionary*, ed. Rado Pribic. New York and London: Garland Publishing, 1990: 251–257.

—— 'The 1988 Nobel Prize in Literature: Najib Mahfuz', *Dictionary of Literary Biography Yearbook*. Detroit: Gale Research Co., 1988: 3–12.

—— 'Najib Mahfuz in World Literature', *The Arabic Novel Since 1950: Critical Essays, Interviews, and Bibliography*, ed. Issa J. Boullata. Vol. 5 of *Mundus Arabicus*. Cambridge: Dar Mahjar, 1992: 121–141.

—— 'Naguib Mahfouz and the Arabic Novel: The Historical Context', *BHNM*: 28–36.

—— 'PROTA: The Project for the Translation of Arabic', *Middle East Studies Association Bulletin* 28 (1994): 165–168.

Altoma, Salih J., 'Najib Mahfuz: A Profile and a Bibliography of Selected Readings', *Middle Eastern Studies Program Newsletter*. Indiana University, Spring 1989: 15–20.

—— 'Naguib Mahfouz: A Profile', *International Fiction Review* 17 (1990): 128–132.

—— *Modern Arabic Poetry in English Translation: A Bibliography* Tangiers: King Fahd School of Translation, 1993.

Altorki, Soraya, 'Patriarchy and Imperialism: Father–Son and British Relations in Najib Mahfuz's Trilogy', *Intimate Selving in Arab Families: Gender, Self, and Identity*, ed. Suad Joseph. Syracuse, NY: Syracuse University Press, 1999: 214–234.

Amyuni, Mona Takieddine, 'Women in Contemporary Arabic and Francophone Fiction', *Feminist Issues* 12: 2 (1992): 3–19.

Appignanesi, Lisa and Sara Maitland, eds, *The Rushdie File* Syracuse, NY: Syracuse University Press, 1990: 42, 141–143, 186–187 [On Mahfuz's views, his censored work *Children of Gebelawi* and India's initial reception of Mahfuz].

Asfour, Gaber, 'From 'Naguib Mahfouz's Critics", trans. Ayman A. el-Desouky. *BHNM*: 144–171.

'Atiyya, Ahmad Muhammad, 'Naguib Mahfouz and the Short Story', trans. Trevor LeGassick, *CPNM*: 9–25.

Barakat, Halim, *The Arab World* Berkeley, CA: University of California Press, 1993: especially 216–223 [Repeats much of the author's 1977 study listed above in the section Pre-1988].

Beard, Michael and Adnan Haydar, eds, *Naguib Mahfouz from Regional Fame to Global Recognition* Syracuse, NY: Syracuse University Press, 1993.

—— 'The Mahfouzian Sublime', *BHNM*: 95–104.

—— See Haydar, Adnan.

Bloom, Harold, *The Western Canon* New York: Harcourt, Brace, 1994 [Note Appendix D: The Chaotic Age, which lists, from Arabic, Mahfuz's *Midaq Alley*, *Fountain and Tomb* and *Miramar* in addition to one title each by the Arab authors Adunis, Mahmud Darwish and Taha Husayn].

Bowles, Paul, see Abdel-Jaouad, Hedi and al-Misbahi, Hassuna.

Chevalier, Tracy, ed., *Contemporary World Writers*. Second edition. Detroit, MI: St James Press, 1993: 337–339.

Coetzee, J. M., 'Fabulous Fabulist', *The New York Review of Books* September 22, 1994: 30–33 [A general review of Mahfuz's works with special emphasis on *The Harafish*].

Cole, Gregory, 'Conversation with Mahfouz', *Africa Report* May–June 1990: 65–66.

Cooke, Miriam, 'Naguib Mahfouz: Review Article', *Middle East Journal* 43 (1989): 507–511 [Reviews primarily *The Search* and *Fountain and Tomb*].

—— 'Men Constructed in the Mirror of Prostitution', *BHNM*: 106–125.

—— 'Naguib Mahfouz, Men, and the Egyptian Underworld', *Fictions of Masculinity: Crossing Cultures, Crossing Sexualities*, ed. Peter F. Murphy. New York: New York University Press, 1994: 96–120.

Corsaro, Julie, 'Arabic Materials and Programs', *Venture into Cultures*, ed. Carla Hayden. Chicago: American Library Association, 1992: especially 19–21.

D'Souza, Dinesh, 'Multiculturalism 101: Great Books of the Non-Western World', *Policy Review* 56 (Spring 1991): 22–30, especially 29.

DeYoung, Terri, '*Midaq Alley* by Najib Mahfuz', *African Literature and Its Times*, Eds Joyce Moss and Lorraine Valestuk, Detroit, MI: Gale, 2000: 259–268.

Dickey, Christopher, 'A Baedeker to Egypt's Soul: Mahfouz's Masterpiece Is Published in English', *Newsweek* February 26, 1990: 64.

—— 'At the Ali Baba Cafe', *Vanity Fair* November 1989: 234–244, 258.

—— and Theodore Stanger, 'Have We Got a Deal for You', *Newsweek* November 11, 1991: 36.

Elad, Ami, 'Mahfuz's 'Za'balawi': Six Stations of a Quest', *International Journal of Middle East Studies* 26 (1994): 631–644.

Elbarabry, Samir, 'Mahfuz's *Midaq Alley* and Hardy's *The Return of the Native*: Some Parallels', *Al-'Arabiyya* 28 (1995): 81–94.

El-Enany, Rasheed, 'The Dichotomy of Islam and Modernity in the Fiction of Naguib Mahfouz', *The Postcolonial Crescent: Islam's Impact on Contemporary Literature*, John C. Hawley (ed.), New York: P. Lang, 1998: 79–83.

—— 'Mahfouz: A Great Novel and a Wanting Translation', *Third World Quarterly*, 13 (1992): 187–189. [On the English translation of Mahfuz's *Palace Walk*.]

Espmark, Kjell, *The Nobel Prize in Literature: A Study of the Criteria behind the Choices* [An English translation of the author's Swedish work prepared by the publisher on the basis of a translation provided by Robin Fulton and Kjell Espmark] Boston, MA: G. K. Hall, 1991: 132, 142–143, 158, 162.

Fadiman, Clifton, ed., *The World of the Short Story: A Twentieth Century Collection* New York: Avenel Books, 1990. The first edition was published in 1986, Boston: Houghton Mifflin.

Fein, Esther B., 'Egyptian Nobel Winner Criticizes *Satanic Verses*', *New York Times* August 5, 1992: B3.

Fox, Edward, 'The Watcher on the Curb', *ARAMCO* March–April 1989: 17–19.

al-Ghitani, Gamal, 'From 'Naguib Mahfouz Remembers'', trans. Mona N. Mikhail, *BHNM*: 28–36.

Gordimer, Nadine, 'The Dialogue of Late Afternoon', *Salmagundi* 113 (1997): 166–173 [Deals with Mahfuz's *Echoes of an Autobiography*].

Gordon, Haim, 'Education for Peace and the Reading of Literature', *The Centennial Review* 34 (1990): 577–586.

—— *Naguib Mahfouz's Egypt: Existential Themes in his Writings* New York: Greenwood, 1990.

Hampl, Patricia, ed., *The Houghton Mifflin Anthology of Short Fiction* Boston, MA: Houghton Mifflin, 1989.

Hartman, Michelle, 'Re-reading Women into Naguib Mahfouz's al-Liss wa'l-kilab (*The Thief and the Dogs*)', *Research in African Literature* 28, 3 (1997): 5–16.

Hassan, Ihab, 'The First Arab Laureate', *The World and I* 5 (1990): 357–366.

Haydar, Adnan and Michael Beard, 'Mapping the World of Naguib Mahfouz', *BHNM*: 1–9.

—— See Beard, Michael and Adnan Haydar.

Hedges, Chris, 'Novelist's Unwitting Role: Sword against Militants', *New York Times* November 15, 1994: A4.

Horwitz, Tony, *Baghdad without a Map and Other Misadventures in Arabia* New York: Dutton, 1991: especially 12.

Hower, Edward, '*Palace Walk* by Naguib Mahfouz', *New York Times Book Review* 3 February 1990: 11.

Hutchins, William M., 'Mahfuz, Nagib', *Contemporary World Writers*. Second edition, ed. Tracy Chevalier. Detroit, MI: St James Press, 1993: 337–339.

Jayyusi, Salma Khadra, 'The Arab Laureate and the Road to Nobel', *BHNM*: 10–20.

—— 'The Nobel Laureate', Introduction to *Midaq Alley*. Washington, DC: Three Continents Press, 1990: v–xv.

Kearns, George, 'Fiction: In History and Out', *The Hudson Review* 44 (1991): 491–499, especially 491–493 [Review of Mahfuz's *Palace of Desire* and *Palace Walk*].

Kessler, Brad, 'Laureate in the Land of the Pharaohs', *New York Times Magazine* June 3, 1990: 39, 60–62, 68–70, 80.

Khoury, Mousa, 'Salvation and the Negativist', trans. Trevor LeGassick, *CPNM*: 37–49.

Lawall, Sarah, 'Naguib Mahfouz and the Nobel Prize: Reciprocal Expectations', *BHNM*: 21–27.

LeGassick, Trevor, 'The Arabic Novel in English Translation', *The Arabic Novel since 1950: Critical Essays, Interviews, and Bibliography*, ed. Issa J. Boullata. Vol. 5 of *Mundus Arabicus*. Cambridge: Dar Mahjar, 1992: 47–60, especially 52–53.

—— ed., *Critical Perspectives on Naguib Mahfouz*, Washington, DC: Three Continents Press, 1991.

—— 'The Faith of Islam in Modern Arabic Fiction', *Religion and Literature* 20 (1988): 92–109, especially 100–104.

—— 'False Values', *The World and I* September 1990: 392–397 [Based on the author's reading of Mahfuz's *Autumn Quail*, *The Beggar* and *Respected Sir*].

—— 'Postface', *Miramar*. Second edition. Washington, DC: Three Continents Press, 1990: 143–156.

—— 'Trials of Faith', *The World and I* 5 (1990): 367–379.

—— 'Trials of the Flesh and of the Intellect', *The World and I* February 1992: 424–431 [Based on the author's reading of Mahfuz's *Midaq Alley*, *Palace of Desire* and *Sugar Street*].

Lipson, Eden Ross, 'The Nobel Effect', *New York Times Book Review* February 4, 1990: 11 [A brief note].

Loughery, John, ed., *Into the Widening World: International Coming-of-Age Stories* New York: Persea, 1994 [Includes Mahfuz's 'The Conjuror Made off with the Dish'].

Love, Kennett, 'How I Won the Nobel Prize (for Naguib Mahfouz)', *Poets and Writers* 17: 4 (1989): 17–22.

Lundquist, Suzanne Evertsen, 'Narrative Theory in Naguib Mahfouz's *The Children of Gebelawi*', *Understanding Others: Cultural and Cross-Cultural Studies and the Teaching of* Literature, eds Joseph Trimmer and Tilly Warnock. Urbana, IL: National Council of Teachers of English, 1992: 213–229.

Luxner, Larry, 'A Nobel for the Arab Nation', *ARAMCO* March–April 1989: 14–16.

Lyons, Robert, 'View from a Cairo Roof', *New York Times Magazine* August 23, 1992: 34.

McDermott, Anthony, *Egypt from Nasser to Mubarak: A Flawed Revolution* London and New York: Croom Helm, 1988: 23, 234–236.

Mack, Maynard, ed., 'Naguib Mahfouz', *The Norton Anthology of World Masterpieces*. Vol. 2. New York: W. W. Norton, 1992: 1961–1964 (on Mahfuz) and 1965–1973 ('Zaabalawi').

Madden, David, ed., *The World of Fiction* Fort Worth, TX: Holt, Rinehart and Winston, 1990: 645–649.

Magrath, Douglas R., 'Arabic Fiction: Tradition, Modernism, and Social Change', *Muslim World* 80 (1990): 190–205.

'Mahfouz, Naguib', *Current Biography Yearbook* 50 (1989): 365–369.

Mahfuz, Najib, 'Khomeini is a Terrorist' [An English translation of *Der Spiegel*'s interview with Mahfuz in 1989] in *The Rushdie File*, eds Lisa Appignanesi and Sara Maitland. Syracuse, NY: Syracuse University Press, 1990: 140–142.

—— *The Nobel Lecture*, trans. Muhammad Salamawy [The Arabic and English texts]. Cairo: AUCP, 1988.

—— 'The Nobel Lecture'. Reprinted in *Poets and Writers* July–August 1989: 13–16, and in *Dictionary of Literary Biography Yearbook*, Detroit: Gale Research Co., 1988: 12–14.

—— See El-Shabrawy below.

Makar, Ragai N., *Naguib Mahfouz, a Bibliography: Arabic, English, French* Salt Lake City, UT: University of Utah Libraries, Special Collection, Middle East Library, 1990.

Mallory, Carole, 'Mailer and Vidal: The Big Schmooze', *Esquire* May 1991: 105–112.

Malti-Douglas, Fedwa, 'Mahfouz's Dream', *BHNM*: 126–143.

Matar, Nabil I., 'Homosexuality in the Early Novels of Nageeb Mahfouz', *Journal of Homosexuality* 26 (1994): 77–90.

Mehrez, Samia, *Egyptian Writers between History and Fiction: Essays on Naguib Mahfouz, Sonallah Ibrahim, and Gamal al-Ghitani* Cairo: AUCP, 1994.

—— 'Respected Sir', *BHNM*: 52–60.

Meredith, Don, 'Looking for Sugar Street', *Texas Review* 18.3–4 (1997): 83–95.

Mikhail, Mona, 'Existential Themes in a Traditional Cairo Setting.' *BHNM*: 81-94.

—— 'Naguib Mahfouz: The Nobel Prize Laureate in Literature, 1988', *Newsletter of the American Research Center in Egypt* 142 (1988): 1–5.

—— *Studies in the Short Fiction of Mahfouz and Idris* New York: New York University Press, 1992.

Milson, Menahem, 'A Great 20th Century Novelist', *Commentary* June 1991: 34–38.

al-Misbahi, Hassuna, 'al-Amriki alladhi katab 'an Tanja' (The American who wrote about Tangiers), *al-Majalla* December 7–12, 1988: 66–70 [An interview with Paul Bowles, which includes Bowles's cryptic reference to Mahfuz].

Montiero, George, 'The Trick in Naguib Mahfouz's 'Half a Day'', *Notes on Contemporary Literature* 33.5 (2003): 2–3.

Moosa, Matti, *The Early Novels of Naguib Mahfouz: Images of Modern Egypt* Gainesville, FL: University of Florida Press, 1994.

—— 'Naguib Mahfouz: Life in the Alley of Arab History', *Georgia Review* 49.1 (1995): 224–230.

Morgan, Speer I. et al., eds, *The Best of the Missouri Review: Fiction 1978–1990* Columbia, MO: University of Missouri Press, 1991: 252–260.

al-Nahhas, Hashim, 'The Role of Naguib Mahfouz in the Egyptian Cinema', trans. Trevor LeGassick, *CPNM*: 163–173.

Nashed, Adel, 'Naguib Mahfouz: A Comparison between his Written and Spoken Words', *Bi'l-Arabi/In Plain Arabic* April/May 1990: 57–56.

'Notable Books of 1990', *American Libraries* March 1991: 212.

Powers, John, 'Chronicler of Egypt', *Connoisseur* April 1989: 50, 54.

Raina, M. L. 'Balladist of the Crooked Alley', *Quest* 107 (September–October1994): 111–113.

Roberts, Paul William, *River in the Desert: Modern Travels in Ancient Egypt* New York: Random House, 1993: especially 185–190, 50, 54.

Roded, Ruth, 'Gender in an Allegorical Life of Muhammad: Mahfouz's *Children of Gebelawi*', *Muslim World* 93 (2003): 117–134.

Rodenbeck, John, 'Foreword', *The Beggar*. Third printing, 1988: 5–6.

—— ed. *Reading Egypt: Literature, History, and Culture* Cairo: AUCP, 2000.

Said, Edward, 'Embargoed Literature', *Nation* September 17, 1990: 278–280.

—— 'Goodbye to Mahfuz', *London Review of Books* December 8, 1988: 10–11.

Salmawy, Mohammed, 'Nobel Lecture, 8 December 1988', *Georgia Review* 49.1 (1995): 220–223.

El-Shabrawy, Charlotte, 'Naguib Mahfouz: The Art of Fiction' [Interview], *Paris Review* Summer 1992: 51–73.

Shammas, Anton, 'Introduction', *The Middle East, Michigan Quarterly Review* [Special issue] 31 (1992): 253–256.

—— 'The Shroud of Mahfouz', *The New York Review of Books* February 2, 1989: 19–21.

Shasha, David, 'Betool Khedairi's *A Sky So Close*', *Sephardic Heritage Update Online*. No.14 July 20, 2001.

al-Shaykh, Hanan, see Sunderman, Paula W.

Shepard, William, 'Satanic Verses and the Death of God: Salman Rushdie and Najib Mahfuz', *The Muslim World* 82 (1992): 91–111.

'Summer Reading: Recommended Books by African American Writers and English Professors', *American Visions* June 1993: 34–39, especially 39 [Thulani Davis's reference to Mahfuz].

Steif, William, 'Naguib Mahfouz: Fifteen Minutes with Egypt's Nobel Laureate', *The Progressive* 53.2 (1989): 38–39.

Stock, Raymond, 'A Fulbright Year with Naguib Mahfouz', *The Fulbrighter* (Newsletter of the Fulbright Alumni Association) Cairo (Fall 1994): 8–9 [Stock reports on his efforts to write a biography of Mahfuz].

—— 'Naguib Mahfouz: A Translator's View', *Kenyon Review* 23.2 (Spring 2001): 136–142.

Sunderman, Paula W., 'An Interview with Hanan Al-Shaykh', *Michigan Quarterly Review* 31 (1992): 625–636.

al-Tawati, Mustafa, 'Place in Three Novels by Mahfouz', trans. Trevor LeGassick, *CPNM*: 71–83.

Theroux, Peter, 'Children of the Alley: A Translator's Tale', *Massachusetts Review* 42.4 (2001): 666–671.

Viorst, Milton, 'Man of the Gamaliya', *New Yorker* 2 July 1990: 32–52.

—— *Sandcastles: The Arabs in Search of the Modern World* New York: Alfred A. Knopf, 1994: especially 83–121 [On Mahfuz].

Weaver, Mary Ann, 'The Novelist and the Sheikh', *New Yorker* 30 January 1995: 52–69. [On the stabbing of Mahfuz and other issues relevant to Egypt's current political life].

Weigel, George, 'Religion and Peace: An Argument Complexified', *The Washington Quarterly* Spring 1991:2: 7–41, especially 37–39.

CHAPTER TWO

Arabic Fiction, 1947–2003:
An Overview

Before 1988, the year Najib Mahfuz was awarded the Nobel Prize for Literature, the demand for and interest in Arabic fiction was confined to a relatively limited audience. Since then, however, Western publishers and readers have shown a steadily growing interest in contemporary Arabic fiction. Reviewing English translations of contemporary Arabic fiction, it is possible in retrospect to outline their progress in three phases: 1947–1967, 1968–1988 and 1988 onwards.

1947–1967

Western readers showed little interest in works of fiction written in Arabic, whether as translations or as literary studies. This can be explained in part by two facts. First the novel and the short story, like drama, have begun to evolve as genres in Arabic only since the mid-nineteenth century, largely as a result of European influence. Second, Orientalists have, even as late as the 1970s, continued to express reservations about the literary value or the maturity of dramatic or fictional works produced by Arab writers. H. A. R. Gibb, for example, while noting the positive progress made by Arab writers in these genres, felt that their productions, 'short stories, novels, and plays, remain bounded by the horizons and conventions of the Arab world' and that, 'when translated into other languages they are often more interesting as social documents than as literary achievements' (Gibb 1963: 161). As Trevor LeGassick has suggested, other Orientalists have expressed similar views until recent years (LeGassick 1992: 47). Indeed, the most prolific translator of Arabic literature, Denys Johnson-Davies, developed this interest in translation mainly because 'the modern Arabic literary movement was almost neglected

54

by Arabists' (Johnson-Davies 1983: 80). Between the 1947 and 1967 publication dates of Johnson-Davies's first and second translations of Arabic fiction (*Tales from Egyptian Life* by Mahmud Taymur and an anthology of *Modern Arabic Short Stories*), only a small number of works of fiction (perhaps no more than sixteen) appeared in English. This was partly because of the difficulty of finding a publisher for Arabic literary works, as Johnson-Davies himself noted, and, more importantly, the marginal status assigned to modern Arabic literature in general in Oriental or Middle Eastern studies. This phase was also marked by the first appearance in English of any novel by Najib Mahfuz, namely *Midaq Alley*, translated by Trevor LeGassick and published in Beirut in 1966. Other notable translations that appeared during this phase were Tawfiq al-Hakim's *Maze of Justice* (translated by Abba Eban) and *Bird of the East* (translated by R. Bayly Winder) and Abd al-Rahman al-Sharqawi's *Egyptian Earth* (translated by Desmond Stewart).

1968–1988

A phase of expanding, but largely academic interest, this period was marked by a more active and continuous effort to translate modern Arabic literature in general, and modern Arabic fiction in particular. Not only did a much larger number of works of fiction appear in English translation (some sixty novels and forty anthologies of short stories), representing a greater number of Arab authors, but there also emerged numerous relevant studies, which contributed to a broader understanding and appreciation of Arabic fiction. The number of academic and non-academic translators likewise increased, Johnson-Davies being notable for his numerous, highly successful and well-received translations. In addition to his earlier two works, he translated about ten novels and anthologies of short stories, including some of the finest that appeared in Arabic, such as Tayyib Salih's *Season of Migration to the North*, published in 1969 and reprinted at least seven times up to 2003.

Geographical Representation

In terms of their geographical scope, these translations represented mostly Egyptian writers but included a few works by other noted Arab novelists: Tawfiq Awwad and Halim Barakat (Lebanon), Jabra I. Jabra and Ghassan Kanafani (Palestine), Abd al-Rahman Munif (Jordan/Saudi Arabia), Tayyib Salih (Sudan) and Muhammad Shukri (Morocco). Of all Arab writers, it was Najib Mahfuz who became the focus of successive studies and translations.

However, most of his translated works were initially published in Cairo (by the American University in Cairo Press). The most notable exception was his allegorical and highly controversial novel *Children of Gebelawi* (1981), which was published in London and Washington.

Arab Women Writers

Another positive trend that began to emerge during this period was the translation of books by Arab women writers, such as Sahar Khalifah (1985), Emily Nasrallah (1987), Alifa Rifaat (1983), Nawal Sa'dawi (1983, 1985, 1987, 1988) and Hanan al-Shaykh (1986). The number of translated works by these and other women writers increases as we proceed beyond the 1980s. This growing interest in women's writings can be explained by two facts. First, more talented Arab women writers have emerged and made significant contributions to Arabic literature during the last four decades. Second, the global orientation of feminism in the West has brought into focus the cause of feminism in developing countries and women's perspectives about major political and social issues in their respective countries. Of all Arab women writers, Sa'dawi has undoubtedly been the most widely represented (by at least seven translations) and has received the most favourable reviews in feminist literature. This is due perhaps more to her radical and outspoken portrayal of women's conditions in Egypt and Arab societies than to the intrinsic literary value of her works. Though censored or banned in Egypt and elsewhere in the region, Sa'dawi's works, both fiction and non-fiction, have received wide circulation in the West, reaching beyond the usually limited audience that Arabic literature enjoyed up until 1988. As the Egyptian critic Sabry Hafez noted in his 1989 review, Sa'dawi as a novelist 'is by no means the best female Arab writer' (Hafez 1989: 188). Others such as Amal Amireh attribute Sa'dawi's reputation to her focus on themes that confirm Western stereotypes about the Arab world.[1] There are other women novelists, in Egypt or elsewhere, who were either overlooked or marginally represented in this period, including Sa'dawi's compatriots Latifah al-Zayyat (1923–1996) and Radwa Ashur. The translations of some of al-Zayyat's works began to appear only in the late 1990s, her *The Owner of the House* being published in 1997 and *The Open Door* in 2000, whereas Ashur's only translated novel, *Granada*, was

---

1. Amal Amireh, ' Framing Nawal El Saadawi: Arab Feminism in a Transnational World', *Intersections: Gender, Nation, and Community in Arab Women's Novels*, ed. Lisa Suhair Majaj, Paula W. Sunderman and Therese Saliba. Syracuse, NY: Syracuse University Press, 2002: 33– 67.

published in 2003. It is important to add that short stories by Arab women began to appear in anthologies as early as 1967.

1988–2003

The post-Nobel phase represents, in several ways, a striking departure from the earlier phases. The first obvious development is the relative frequency and regularity with which Arabic works of fiction were translated or reprinted in response to demands. Note, for example, the various editions and printings of works by Mahfuz, Munif, Sa'dawi, Salih and Shaykh. Second, a larger number of publishers, including, for the first time, major commercial publishers and university presses, have become involved in the publishing and marketing of contemporary Arabic works. Special reference should be made to the series that the Three Continents Press and PROTA (Project for Translation from Arabic) founded by Salma Khadra Jayyusi[1] have published or sponsored in the US, and the several more recent series being put out by such American university presses and programmes as Arkansas, Columbia, Minnesota, Texas and the University of Texas's Center for Middle Eastern Studies. To these must be added the effective role that the mainstream journals have exercised in expanding the audience for Arabic literature. Such journals, especially library-oriented journals, have begun to review on a fairly regular basis Arabic works in English translation, and to recommend them for acquisition by public libraries.

In short, by the end of the twentieth century, an extensive corpus of Arabic fiction has become accessible in English translation to an equally expanded

1. Three Continents Press is particularly noted, more than any other publishing institution, for its pioneering role in promoting the translation of modern Arabic literature. For more detailed information, see Donald E. Herdeck, *Appreciating the Difference: The Autobiography of Three Continents Press: 1973–1997*Pueblo, CO: Passeggiata Press, 1998. See especially pp. 31–39, 82–90 and 94–114. Publications sponsored by PROTA cover different genres or periods of Arabic literature including modern fiction, as represented in the following works: *The Secret Life of Saeed, the Ill-Fated Pessoptimist* by Emile Habibi (1982), *Wild Thorns* by Sahar Khalifah (1985), *War in the Land of Egypt* by Yusuf al-Qa'id (1986), *All That's Left to You and Other Stories* by Ghassan Kanafani (1990), *The Sheltered Quarter* by Hamza Bogary (1991), *A Balcony over the Fakihani* by Liyanah Badr (1993), *Prairies of Fever* by Ibrahim Nasr Allah (1993), *Fragments of Memory* by Hanna Mina (1993),*The Hostage* by Zayd Muti' Dammaj (1994), *The Lake* by Yahya Yakhlif (1999), *The Bleeding of the Stone* by Ibrahim al-Kuni (2002) and *The Tree and Other Stories* by Abd Allah al-Nasir (2003). PROTA's other anthologies that include works of fiction are: *Literature of Modern Arabia* (1988) and *Anthology of Modern Palestinian Literature* (1992). What is noteworthy about PROTA's publications is that they have received favourable reviews in American mainstream journals.

audience. The corpus is largely representative of contemporary Arabic fiction in terms of major themes, trends, works and authors, but it continues to show a skewed pattern of representation resulting from the predominance of Egyptian authors.[1] There are several reasons for this preponderance. First among them is the fact that Egypt has, since the beginning of the nineteenth century, assumed a leading role in the development of Arabic literature. As a result, Arabists have, on the whole, focused more on Egypt than on other Arab countries. Second, the translation and printing of Egyptian works have been promoted through active support by such institutions, Egyptian and non-Egyptian, as the Ministry of Culture's General Egyptian Book Organization (known for its series on 'Contemporary Arabic Literature'), the American University in Cairo Press, the American Research Center in Egypt and York Press (Canada). The emphasis on Egypt is undoubtedly justified but should not continue to exclude the many talented writers, both men and women, from other Arab countries (Algeria, Iraq, Lebanon, Morocco, Syria, Tunisia, etc.) who have made notable contributions to Arabic fiction. For lack of space, only few names can be cited here under their respective countries:

Algeria	Wasini al-A'raj, Muhammad al-Ali 'Ar'ar, Isma'il Ghamuqat, Abd al-Hamid bin Hadduqah, al-Habib al-Sa'ih, al-Tahir Wattar;
Bahrain	Muhammad Abd al-Malik, Abd al-Qadir 'Aqil, Ali Abd Allah Khalifah;
Iraq	Dhu'l Nun Ayyub, Ghazi al-Abbadi, Ghanim al-Dabbagh, Lutfiyyah al-Dulaymi, Gha'ib Tu'mah Farman, Burhan al-Khatib, Muhammad Khudayyir, Shakir Khusbak, Samirah al-Mani', Abd al-Malik Nuri, Ali al-Qasimi, Abd al-Rahman al-Rubay'i, Mahdi 'Isa al-Saqr;
Kuwait	Isma'il Fahd Isma'il, Sulayman al-Shatti, Layla Uthman;
Lebanon	Yusuf al-Ashqar, Layla Ba'labakki, Suhayl Idris;

1. The predominance of Egyptian authors is illustrated by the fact that most of the 322 titles listed in the bibliography below (about 170 titles) are Egyptian. The remaining titles represent: Algeria (2), Iraq (11), Jordan (3), Kuwait (1), Lebanon (26), Libya (7), Morocco (8), Palestine (22), Saudi Arabia (11), Sudan (5), Syria (11), (3), Tunisia (2), United Arab Emirates and Yemen (2). About twenty other collections are noted for their attempt to represent authors from several Arab countries. Two of the best examples are the first pioneering pan-Arab anthology, *Modern Arabic Short Stories* (1967), and the more recent collection, *Under the Naked Sky: Short Stories from the Arab World* (2000) both of which were edited and translated by Denys Johnson-Davies.

Morocco	Khanathah Binnunh, Abd al-Karim Ghallab, Idris al-Khuri, Abdallah Laroui, Ahmad al-Madini, Mubarak Rabi', Muhammad 'Izz al-Din al-Tazi, Muhammad Zifzaf;
Palestine	Samirah Azzam;
Saudi Arabia	Raja' al-'Alim, Muhammad Alwan, Khalil al-Fuzay', Husayn Ali Husayn, Abd al-Aziz al-Mishri, Ibrahim al-Nasir, Khayriyyah al-Saqqaf;
Syria	Walid Ikhlasi, Kulit al-Khuri, Hani al-Rahib, Abd al-Salam al-'Ujayli;
Tunisia	Salah al-Din Bu Jah, Muhammad Rashad Hamzawi, Muhammad Salih al-Jabiri, al-Bashir Khurayyif, 'Izz al-Din al-Madani, Mahmud al-Mas'adi, al-Arusi al-Matwi;
United Arab Emirates	Abd al-Hamid Ahmad and Muhammad Hasan al-Harbi;
Yemen	Sa'id al-'Awlaqi and Ahamd Mahfuz Umar.

There is also an obvious absence in the translated corpus of writers, such as Najib al-Kilani and Abd al-Hamid Judah al-Sahhar, who tend to represent Islamic themes in their short stories or novels. Furthermore, the translated texts, which both Arab and non-Arab translators have prepared over the last fifty years, have not yet been assessed in systematic studies. The few general observations given in brief reviews do not shed sufficient light on the accuracy or the literary quality of the translated texts or on other issues and aspects relevant to the whole process of selecting and translating specific texts and authors.

Works Cited

Amireh, Amal, 'Remembering Latifa al-Zayyat', *ajadid* 2.12 (1996): 6–7. Zayyat's work cited by Amireh appeared in 1997 under the title *The Owner of the House*, as listed in the bibliography below.

Gibb, H. A. R., *Arab Literature*. Second edition. London: Oxford University Press, 1963.

Hafez, Sabry, 'Intention and Realization in the Narratives of Nawal El-Saadawi', *Third World Quarterly* 11.3 (1989): 188–198.

Johnson-Davies, Denys, 'On Translating Arabic Literature: An Interview with Denys Johnson-Davies', *Alif* 3 (1983): 80–93. Reprinted in *The View from*

Within: Writers and Critics on Contemporary Arabic Literature, ed. Ferial J. Ghazoul and Barbara Harlow. Cairo: AUCP, 1994: 272–282. For his recent remarks about the difficulty he encountered earlier in publishing his translations see 'Translation Is First and Foremost an Art and not a Science', *Banipal* 9 (Autumn 2000): 38–41 [an interview with Margaret Oban] and the anthology he edited and translated, *Under the Naked Sky: Short Stories from the Arab World* Cairo: AUCP, 2000:1–2.

LeGassick, Trevor, 'The Arabic Novel in English Translation', *The Arabic Novel since 1950: Critical Essays, Interviews, and Bibliography*, ed. Issa J. Boullata. Vol. 5 of *Mundus Arabicus*. Cambridge, MA: Dar Mahjar, 1992: 47–60.

CHAPTER THREE

Arabic Fiction in English Translation: A Chronological Bibliography, 1947–2003

This updated bibliography covers translated works published during the period cited. Entries are arranged according to the first edition of each book, with the exception of Taha Husayn's autobiographical novels. However, numerous entries include the year/years of other editions or reprints of the same work. Note for example, under 1947, al-Hakim, *Maze of Justice* London: The Harvill Press; University of Texas Press, 1989; under 1966, Mahfuz, *Midaq Alley*, 1975, 1977, 1981, 1984, 1989 and 1992; under 1969, Salih, *Season of Migration to the North*, where reference is made to editions that appeared in 1970, 1976, 1980, 1984, 1989, 1991, 1997 and 2003; and, under 1986, al-Shaykh, *The Story of Zahra*, for references to other editions of 1991, 1994 and 1995. The author's country of origin is indicated in the case of non-Egyptians only by the abbreviations listed below. Items by Egyptian authors are not marked. Short-story collections are identified by (*) and their contents are provided in selected cases. Note, for example, entry no.16, *Modern Arabic Short Stories*, trans. Denys Johnson-Davies, where reference is made to writers who are represented. With a few exceptions (Taha Husayn, Nawal al- Sa'dawi, Muhammad Shukri and others), the bibliography does not cover autobiographical works or works by Arab authors originally written in English, French or other languages. Nor does it cover the works of Moroccan storytellers, which have been translated by Paul Bowles. The latter are based on recordings transmitted in the Moroccan vernacular, for which no written texts have been printed. English translations of Francophone North African writers or of juvenile fiction written in Arabic are also excluded. The latter includes works such as Zakariya Tamir's *The Horse of the Green Land* and *The Horse and the Merchant* translated by Denys Johnson-Davies. Several international anthologies, which include selections from modern Arabic fiction, have been added only as a partial guide to the place or reception of Arabic literature in recent anthologies of world literature (see entries numbers 138, 193, 198, 210, 214, 263, 268 and 272). These are marked by (**).

Abbreviations

A = Algeria; AW = works representing several Arab countries; I = Iraq; J = Jordan; K= Kuwait; L = Lebanon; Li = Libya; M = Morocco; P = Palestine; S = Syria; SA = Saudi Arabia; SU = Sudan; T = Tunisia; U = United Arab Emirates; Y = Yemen.

AUCP = The American University in Cairo Press.

GEBO = General Egyptian Book Organization, Ministry of Culture, Cairo.

1947

1. al-Hakim, Tawfiq, *Maze of Justice*, trans. Abba Eban. London: The Harvill Press, 1980; Austin, TX: University of Texas Press, 1989; London: Saqi, 1989.

2. *Taymur, Mahmud, *Tales from Egyptian Life*, trans. Denys Johnson-Davies. Cairo: Renaissance Bookshop.

1948

3. Husayn, Taha, The Stream of Days: A Student at the Azhar, trans. Hilary Wayment. London: Longman, Green. See earlier edition Cairo: al-Maaref, 1943.

1952

4. Nu'aymah, Mikha'il, *The Memoirs of a Vagrant Soul, or The Pitted Face*, New York: Philosophical Library. (L)

1957

5. *Nu'aymah, Mikha'il, *Till We Meet and Twelve Other Stories* Bangalore, India: Indian Institute of World Affairs. (L)

1959

6. Husayn, Muhammad Kamil, *City of Wrong: A Friday in Jerusalem*, trans. Kenneth Cragg. London: G. Bles; New York: Seabury Press, 1966; Oxford; Rockport, MA: Oneworld, 1994.

1961

7. *Modern Egyptian Short Stories*, trans. Louis Morcos. Cairo: The Anglo–Egyptian Bookshop [Includes stories by Abbas Ahmad, Yahya Haqqi, Yusuf Idris, Ibrahim al-Mazini, Abd al-Mun'im Salim, Yusuf Sharuni and Abd Allah al-Tukhi].

1962

8. al-Sharqawi, 'Abd al-Rahman, *Egyptian Earth*, trans. Desmond Stewart. London: Heinemann, 1962; Delhi: Hind Pocket Books; Delhi: Hind Pockets Books, 1972; London: Saqi, 1990; Austin, TX: University of Texas Press, 1990.

1964

9. *Rushdi, Rashad, *Selected Stories and Essays* Cairo: The Anglo–Egyptian Bookshop [Includes six short stories].

10. Taymur, Mahmud, *The Call of the Unknown*, trans. Hume Horan. Beirut: Khayats.

1965

11. Damanhuri, Hamid, *The Price of Sacrifice*, trans. Ghida Shahbandar. Beirut: Khayats. (SA)

1966

12. Ghanim, Fathi, *The Man Who Lost his Shadow*, trans. Desmond Stewart. Boston, MA: Houghton Mifflin; London and Washington, DC: Heinemann Educational Books and Three Continents Press, 1980; Cairo: AUCP, 1994.

13. al-Hakim, Tawfiq, *Bird of the East*, trans. R. Bayly Winder. Beirut: Khayats.

14. Mahfuz, Najib, *Midaq Alley*, trans. Trevor Le Gassick. Beirut: Khayats. Revised edition. London: Heinemann Educational Books, 1975; Washington, DC: Three Continents Press, 1977, 1981, 1989; Cairo: AUCP, 1984, New York: Anchor Books, 1992.

1967

15. Mahmud, Mustafa, *The Rising from the Coffin*, trans. David Bishai. Revised by Farouk Abdel Wahab. Cairo: [GEBO? Arab Writer Publishers and Printers?].

16. *Modern Arabic Short Stories*, trans. Denys Johnson-Davies. London: Oxford University Press; Heinemann Educational Books, 1974, 1976, 1980; Washington, DC: Three Continents Press, 1981, 1984; Cairo: AUCP, 1993 [Includes stories by Shukri Ayyad, Layla Ba'labakki, Mahmud Diyab, Tawfiq al-Hakim, Yahay Haqqi, Yusuf Idris, Walid Ikhlasi, Jabra Ibrahim Jabra, Ghassan Kanafani, Tu'ma al-Khuri, Najib Mahfuz, Abd al-Malik Nuri, Tayyib Salih, Abd al-Mun'im Salim, Yusuf Sharuni, Fu'ad Takarli, Zakariya Tamir, Mahmud Taymur, Abd al-Salam al-Ujayli, Latifah al-Zayyat]. (AW)

1968

17. **Arabic Writing Today: The Short Story*, ed. Mahmoud Manzalaoui. Cairo: American Research Center in Egypt. Reprinted as *Arabic Short Stories: 1945–1965* Cairo: AUCP, 1985. [Includes short stories by Ihsan Abd al-Quddus, Shukri Ayyad, Samirah Azzam, Ala' Dib, Abd al-Rahman Fahmi, Sulayman Fayyad, Fathi Ghanim, Tawfiq al-Hakim, Ghalib Halasa, Yahya Haqqi, Muhammad Kamil Husayn, Yusuf Idris, Ihsan Kamal, Hasib Kayyali, Idwar Kharrat, Faruq Khurshid, Najib Mahfuz, Suhayr Qalamawi, Muhammad Hafiz Rajab, Rashad Mahmud Rushdi, Mahmoud Sa'dani, Abd al-Qadir Samihi, Ghadah Samman, Abd al-Rahman Sharqawi, Diya' Sharqawi, Yusuf Sharuni, Yusuf Siba'i, Zakariya Tamir, Mahmud Taymur, Majid Tubya]. (AW)

18. *Salih, Tayeb [al-Tayyib], *The Wedding of Zein and Other Stories*, trans. Denys Johnson-Davies. London, Nairobi: Heinemann Educational Books, 1968, 1970, 1978; Portsmouth, NH: Heinemann, 1988; Washington, DC: Three Continents Press, 1968, 1985, Boulder, CO: Lynne Rienner, 1999. (SU)

1969

19. Salih, Tayeb, *Season of Migration to the North*, trans. Denys Johnson-Davies. London: Heinemann Educational Books, 1969, 1970, 1976, 1991; Washington, DC: Three Continents Press, 1980, 1984, 1989; New York: M. Kesend, 1989; Boulder, CO: Lynne Rienner, 1997; London: Penguin, 2003. (SU)

1971

20. *Ibrahim, Sun'Allah [Sonallah], *The Smell of it and Other Stories*, trans. Denys Johnson-Davies. London: Heinemann Educational Books, 1971, 1978.

21. **Modern Iraqi Short Stories*, trans. Ali Qasimi and W. McClung Frazier. Baghdad: Ministry of Information. (I)

1972

22. *Mahfuz, Najib, *A Selection of Short Stories* Cairo: Prism Publications.

1973

23. **Afro-Asian Short Stories: An Anthology Cairo: Permanent Bureau of Afro-Asian Writers. 2 vols [Vol. I includes stories from Algeria, Egypt, Morocco, Syria, Tunisia and Yemen. Vol. II includes stories from Egypt, Iraq, Palestine and Sudan]. (AW)

24. *Haqqi, Yahya, *The Saint's Lamp and Other Stories*, trans. M. M. Badawi. Leiden: E. J. Brill.

25. *Mahfuz, Najib, *God's World*, trans. Akef Abadir and Roger Allen. Minneapolis, MN: Bibliotheca Islamica, 1988.

26. Shukri, Muhammad, *For Bread Alone*, trans. Paul Bowles. London: P. Owen; San Francisco: City Lights Books, 1987; London: Saqi, 1993. (M)

27. *al-Siba'i, Yusuf, *The Cobbler and Other Stories*, trans. Nihad A. Salem et al. Cairo: Permanent Bureau of Afro-Asian Writers.

1974

28. Abd Allah, Muhammad Abd al-Halim, *The Searcher for the Truth*, trans. Muhammad Farid Mahrus. Revised by Mahmoud Shoukry. Cairo: Supreme Council for Islamic Affairs [Biographical fiction dealing with Salman al-Farisi, an early companion of the Prophet Muhammad].

29. Barakat, Halim, *Days of Dust*, trans. Trevor LeGassick. Wilmette, IL: Medina Press International; Washington, DC: Three Continents Press, 1983; Boulder, CO: Lynne Rienner, 1997. (L)

30. Husayn, Taha, *The Dreams of Scheherazade*, trans. Magdi Wahba. Cairo: GEBO.

31. *Nu'aymah, Mikha'il, *A New Year: Stories, Autobiography and Poems*, trans. John Perry. Leiden: E. J. Brill. (L)

1976

32. 'Awwad, Tawfiq Yusuf, *Death in Beirut*, trans. Leslie McLoughlin. London: Heinemann Educational Books; Washington, DC, and Colorado Springs, CO: Three Continents Press, 1984, 1995. (L)

33. Husayn, Taha, A Passage to France: The Third Volume of the Autobiography of Taha Husain, trans. Kenneth Cragg. Leiden: Brill. See also *The Days* Cairo: AUCP, 1997, which includes the three parts of Husayn's autobiography translated and published under three titles: *An Egyptian Childhood* (1932) translated by E. H. Paxton, *The Stream of Days* (1948) by Hilary Wayment, and Cragg's *Passage to France*.

34. al-Mazini, Ibrahim 'Abd al-Qadir, *Ibrahim the Writer*, trans. Magdi Wahba. Revised by Marsden Jones. Cairo: GEBO.

1977

35. *Abushwesha, Redwan, *The King of the Dead and Other Libyan Tales*, trans. Macdara Woods. London: Martin Brian and O'Keeffe. (LI)

36. *Arab Stories East and West*, trans. R. W. Ebied and M. J. L. Young. Leeds: Leeds Oriental Society [Includes stories by Abd al-Qadir Abu Harus (Libya), Tawfiq Yusuf Awwad and Khalil Taqi al-Din (Lebanon), Dhu'l-Nun Ayyb (Iraq), Yusuf Idris and Ihsan Abd al-Quddus (Egypt), al-Tabi'i al-Akhdar, Muhammad al-Sahbi al-Hajji, Ali al-Hussi, Mustafa Mada'ini and Mahmud Tarshunah (Tunisia), Ahmad Mustafa al-Hurshani and Muhammad Allal al-Sanhaji (Morocco), Hasan al-Zahir Zarruq and al-Tayyib Zarruq (Sudan]. (AW)

37. el-Lozi, Salim, *The Emigrés: A Novel* London: Allison & Busby. (L)

38. *Mahfuz, Najib, *Mirrors*, trans. Roger Allen. Minneapolis, MN: Bibliotheca Islamica, 1990, Cairo: AUCP, 1999.

39. *Modern Egyptian Short Stories*, trans. Saad El-Gabalawy. Fredericton, NB, Canada: York Press [Short stories by Yusuf Idris and Najib Mahfuz].

1978

40. *ʿAbd al-Qaddus, Ihsan, *I Am Free and Other Stories*, trans. Trevor LeGassick. Cairo: GEBO.

41. al-ʿAqqad, ʿAbbas Mahmud, *Sara*, trans. M. M. Badawi. Cairo: GEBO.

42. *Egyptian Short Stories*, trans. Denys Johnson-Davies. London: Heinemann Educational Books and Three Continents Press; Three Continents Press, 1990, 1995 [Includes stories by Yahya al-Tahir Abd Allah , Ibrahim Aslan, Muhammad al-Bisati, Abd al-Rahman Fahmi, Sulayman Fayyad, Yahya Haqqi, Jamil Atiyah Ibrahim, SunʿAllah Ibrahim, Yusuf Idris, Idwar Kharrat, Lutfi al-Khuli, Najib Mahfuz, Abd al-Hakim Qasim, Yusuf Sharuni, Yusuf al-Sibaʿi and Baha' Tahir].

43. *Idris, Yusuf, *The Cheapest Nights and Other Stories*, trans. Wadida Wassef. London: Heinemann Educational Books and Washington, DC: Three Continents Press; Washington, DC: Three Continents Press, 1989; Cairo: AUCP, 1990; Boulder, CO: Lynne Rienner, 1997.

44. *—— In the Eye of the Beholder. Tales of Egyptian Life*, ed. Roger Allen. Minneapolis, MN: Bibliotheca Islamica.

45. *Kanafani, Ghassan, *Men in the Sun and Other Palestinian Stories*, trans. Hilary Kilpatrick. London and Washington, DC: Heinemann Educational Books and Three Continents Press; Three Continents Press, 1983; Cairo: AUCP, 1991; Three Continents Press, 1995; Boulder, CO: Lynne Rienner, 1997, 1999. (P)

46. Mahfuz, Najib, *Miramar*, trans. Fatma Moussa-Mahmoud. Revised by Maged el Kommous and John Rodenbeck. London: Heinemann Educational Books; Washington, DC: Three Continents Press, 1990; New York: Anchor Books, 1993.

47. *Stars in the Sky of Palestine: Short Stories*, trans. Faris Glubb. Beirut: Palestine Liberation Organization, Foreign Information Department. (P)

1979

48. Elkhadem, Saad, see *Three Contemporary Egyptian Novels* below: 19–67.

49. Mahfuz, Najib, *al-Karnak*. See *Three Contemporary Egyptian Novels* below: 67–132.

50. Muʻalla, Abd al-Amir, *The Long Days*. 3 vols. Vols 1 and 2, trans. Mohieddin Ismail. London: Ithaca Press, 1979–1980. Vol. 3, trans. A. W. Luʼluʼa. Baghdad: Dar al Maʼmun for Translation and Publishing, 1982. (I)

51. *Three Contemporary Egyptian Novels*, trans. Saad El-Gabalawy. Fredericton, NB, Canada: York Press [Includes Saad Elkhadem's *From Travels of the Egyptian Odysseus*, 19–67; Najib Mahfuz's *al-Karnak*, 67–132; and Ismail Waliyy al-Din's *Hommos Akhdar*, 133–184].

52. Waliyy al-Din, Ismaʻil, *Hommos Akhdar*. See *Three Contemporary Egyptian Novels*: 133–184.

1980

53. Bindari, Sami, *The House of Power*, trans. by the author and Mona St. Leger. Boston: Houghton Mifflin; 1998.

54. Husayn, Taha, *The Call of the Curlew*, trans. A. B. as-Safi. Leiden: E. J. Brill; Cairo: Palm Press, 1997.

55. *Modern Arab Stories*, compiled by S. al-Bazzaz. London: Iraqi Cultural Centre [Includes short stories by Yahya Tahir Abd Allah, Samira al-Mana, Dayzi al-Amir, Dhu al-Nun Ayyub, Muhammad Baradah, Saad al-Bazzaz, Ghassan Kanafani, Muhammad Khudayyir, Abd al-Rahman al-Munif, Abd Allah Niyazi, Abd al-Malik Nuri and Zakariya Tamir]. (AW)

56. Muʻalla, Abd al-Amir, The Long Days. Vol. 3. Translated by A. W. Luʼluʼa. Baghdad: Dar al Maʼmun for Translation and Publishing, 1982. (I)

57. Musa, Sabri, *Seeds of Corruption*, trans. Mona N. Mikhail. Boston: Houghton Mifflin; New York: Interlink Books, 2002. For a different translation, see Musa, Sabri under 1995.

58. Salih, Tayeb, *Season of Migration to the North, and The Wedding of Zein* [combined edition]. London: Quartet Books. (SU)

1981

59. Mahfuz, Najib, *Children of Gebelawi*, trans. Philip Stewart. London: Heinemann; Washington, DC: Three Continents Press, 1981; 1988; 1990. Revised and augmented edition Colorado Springs, CO: Three Continents Press, 1995, 1996; Pueblo, CO: Passeggiata Press, 1997, 2000.

60. *Sixteen Sudanese Short Stories*, selected and ed. by Osman Hassan Ahmad. Washington, DC: Embassy of the Democratic Republic of the Sudan, Office of the Cultural Counselor. (SU)

1982

61. *Battlefront Stories from Iraq*, trans. A. W. Lu'lu'a. Baghdad: Dar al-Ma'mun for Translation [Includes a novella by Adil Abd al-Jabbar and short stories by Khudayyir Abd al-Amir, Latif Hasan, Ali Khayyun, Abd al-Sattar Nasir, Abd al-Khaliq Rikabi, Adnan al-Rubay'i and Muhsin al-Thuwaydi]. (I)

62. Habibi, Emile, *The Secret Life of Saeed, the Ill-fated Pessoptimist: A Palestinian Who Became a Citizen of Israel*, trans. Trevor LeGassick and Salma Khadra Jayyusi. New York: Vintage Press; London: Zed Books, 1985; New York: Readers International, 1989; New York: Interlink Books, 2002. (P)

63. Hetata, Sherif, *The Eye with an Iron Lid*, London: Onyx Press.

64. *Selected Egyptian Short Stories*, Rashad Rushdi et al. Cairo: The Anglo–Egyptian Bookshop.

65. *A Selection of Egyptian Short Stories* Giza, Cairo: Egypt Foreign Press and Information Department, Ministry of Culture.

See also al-Mu'alla under 1979.

1983

66. *Arabic Short Stories*, trans. Denys Johnson-Davies. London: Quartet Books; Berkeley: University of California Press, 1994. (AW)

67. al-Mazini, Ibrahim 'Abd al-Qadir, *Al-Mazini's Egypt* [Includes *Midu and His Accomplices* and *Return to a Beginning*], trans. William M. Hutchins. Washington: Three Continents Press.

68. *Rifaat, Alifa, *Distant View of a Minaret and Other Stories*, trans. Denys Johnson-Davies. London: Heinemann, 1983, 1985, 1987; Portsmouth, NH: Heinemann, 1989.

69. al-Sa'dawi, Nawal, *Woman at Point Zero*, trans. Sherif Hetata. London: Zed Books; Atlantic Highlands, NJ: Zed, 1990.

70. *al-Sharuni, Yusuf, *Blood Feud*, trans. Denys Johnson-Davies. London: Heinemann Educational Books; Cairo: AUCP, 1991.

1984

71. *'Abd Allah, Yahya Taher, *The Mountain of Green Tea*, trans. Denys Johnson-Davies. London: Heinemann Educational Books; Cairo: AUCP, 1991.

72. *Idris, Yusuf, *Rings of Burnished Brass: Short Stories*, trans. Catherine Cobham. London: Heinemann Educational Books; Cairo: AUCP, 1990.

73. —— *The Sinners*, trans. Kristin Peterson-Ishaq. Washington, DC, and Colorado Springs, CO: Three Continents Press, 1984; 1995.

74. *Kamil, Mahmud, *Sheikh Mursi Marries the Land: A Collection of Egyptian Short Stories*, trans. Trevor LeGassick et al. Cairo: GEBO.

75. *Kanafani, Ghassan, *Palestine's Children: Short Stories*, trans. Barbara Harlow. London and Washington, DC: Heinemann Educational Books and Three Continents Press. (P) See also Kanafani under 2000.

76. Mahfuz, Najib, *The Beginning and the End*, trans. Ramses Hanna Awad, ed. Mason Rossiter Smith. Cairo: AUCP; New York: Anchor Books and Doubleday, 1989.

77. —— *The Thief and the Dogs*, trans. Trevor LeGassick and Mustafa Badawi. Revised by John Rodenbeck. Cairo: AUCP, 1985; New York; Doubleday, 1991.

78. —— *Wedding Song*, trans. Olive Kenny. Revised by Mursi Saad El Din and John Rodenbeck. Cairo: AUCP, 1985; New York: Doubleday, 1989.

1985

79. *Flights of Fantasy: Arabic Short Stories*, ed. Ceza Kassem and Malek Hashem. Cairo: Elias Modern Publishing House [Includes stories by Yahya al-Tahir Abd Allah, Muhammad Baradah, Emile Habibi, Yusuf Idris, Ghassan Kanafani, Idar al-Kharrat, Barra' al-Khatib, Muhammad Khudayyir, Najib Mahfuz, Shafiq Majar, Hasan Nasr, Yusuf al-Qa'id, Alifa Rifaat (Rif'at), Ghadah al-Samman, Muhammad Shukri, Zakariya Tamir, Majid Tubya]. (AW)

80. Jabra, Jabra Ibrahim, *The Ship*, trans. Adnan Haydar and Roger Allen. Washington, DC: Three Continents Press. (P)

81. Khalifah, Sahar, *Wild Thorns*, trans. Trevor LeGassick and Elizabeth Fernea. London: Saqi, 1989, 2000; New York: Olive Branch Press, 1989; New York: Interlink Books, 2000; 2003. (P)

82. Mahfuz, Najib, *Autumn Quail*, trans. Roger Allen. Cairo: AUCP; New York: Doubleday, 1990.

83. *Manzalaoui, Mahmood, ed., Arabic Short Stories, 1945–1965 Cairo: AUCP. (AW)

84. al-Sa'dawi, Nawal, *God Dies by the Nile*, trans. Sherif Hetata. London and New York: Zed Books, 1999.

85. —— *Two Women in One*, trans. Osman Nusairi and Jana Gough. London: Saqi; Seattle, WA: Women in Translation, 1986, 1991; Saqi: 2003.

86. * Tamir, Zakariya [also known as Tamer, Zakaria], *Tigers on the Tenth Day and Other Stories*, trans. Denys Johnson-Davies. London: Quartet Books. (S)

1986

87. Elkhadem, Saad, *Ulysses's Hallucinations or the Like*, trans. Saad El-Gabalawy. *Three Pioneering Egyptian Novels*. Fredericton, NB, Canada: York Press: 95–120.

88. Ghitani, Jamal. *Incidents in Za'farani Alley*, trans. Peter O. Daniel. Cairo: GEBO.

89. Haqqi, Mahmud Tahir, *The Virgin of Dinshaway*, trans. Saad El Gabalawy. *Three Pioneering Egyptian Novels*. Fredericton, NB, Canada: York Press: 17–48.

90. Hetata, Sherif. *The Net* London: Zed Books.

91. Jalal, Muhammad, *Trial at Midnight*, trans. Nihad Selaiha. Cairo: GEBO.

92. Lashin, Mahmud Tahir, *Eve without Adam*, trans. Saad El Gabalawy. *Three Pioneering Egyptian Novels*. Fredericton, NB, Canada: York Press: 49–94.

93. Mahfuz, Najib, *The Beggar*, trans. Kristin Walker Henry and Nariman Khales Naili.al-Warraki. Cairo: AUCP; New York: Doubleday, 1990; Cairo: AUCP, 2000.

94. —— *Respected Sir*, trans. Rashid Enany. London: Quartet Books; New York: Doubleday, 1990.

95. al-Qaʿid, Muhammad Yusuf, *War in the Land of Egypt*, trans. Olive and Lorne Kenny and Christopher Tingley. London: Saqi; New York: Interlink Books, 1998.

96. al-Shaykh, Hanan, *The Story of Zahra*, trans. Peter Ford. London: Quartet, 1986, 1991; New York: Anchor Books, 1994, 1995. (L)

97. *Three Pioneering Egyptian Novels*, trans. Saad El Gabalawy. Fredericton, NB, Canada: York Press.

1987

98. **Egyptian Tales and Short Stories of the 1970s and 1980s*, ed. William M. Hutchins. Cairo: AUCP [Includes stories by Tharwat Abaza, Wajih Abd al-Hadi, Ibrahim Abd al-Majid, Hasan Abd al-Munʿim, Mahfuz Abd al-Rahman, Salah Abd al-Sayyid, Abu al-Maʾati Abu al-Naja, Naʿim Atiyya, Zahirah al-Biali, Ali Darwish, Jamal al-Ghitani, Abd al-ʿAl al-Hamamisi, Fuʾad Hijazi, Husayn ʿId Huda Jad, Muhammad al-Makhzanji, Fawzi Abd al-Qadir al-Miladi, Muhammad Kamil Muhammad, Sabri Musa, Amirah Nuwayrah, Yusuf al-Qaʾid, Muna Rajab, Zaynab Rushdi, Nawal al-Saʿdawi, Fathi Salamah, Muhammad Salamawi, Ahmad al-Shaykh, Yaʿqub al-Sharuni, Bahaʾ Tahir, Sahar Tawfiq and Taha Wadi].

99. Fahmi, Abdul Rahman, *The Tears of a Nobody*, trans. Nayla Naguib. Cairo: GEBO.

100. **Haqqi, Yahya, *Good Morning! and Other Stories*, trans. Miriam Cooke. Washington, DC: Three Continents Press.

101. Mahfuz, Najib, *The Search*, trans. Mohamed Islam, ed. Magdi Wahba. Cairo: AUCP; New York: Anchor Books, 1991.

102. Munif, Abdelrahman, *Cities of Salt*, trans. Peter Theroux. London and New York: Cape Cod; and Random House; New York: Vintage, 1989; and London: Vintage, 1994. (J/SA)

103. Musa, Sabri. *The Incident*, trans. Hoda Ayyad. Cairo: GEBO.

104. Nasrallah, Emily, *Flight against Time*, trans. Issa J. Boullata. Charlottetown, Prince Edward Island, Canada: Ragweed Press; Austin, TX: Center for Middle Eastern Studies, University of Texas, 1997. (L)

105. al-Qa'id, Yusuf, *News from the Meneisi Farm*, trans. Marie-Therese Abdel-Messih. Cairo: GEBO.

106. Rizq, Abd al-Fattah [also known as Rizk, Abdel Fattah], *Paradise and the Accursed*, trans. Evine Mohamed Hashem. Cairo: GEBO.

107. *al-Sa'dawi, Nawal, *Death of an Ex-Minister*, trans. Shirley Eber. London: Methuen; Minerva, 1992.

108. *—— *She Has No Place in Paradise*, trans. Shirley Eber. London: Methuen; Minerva, 1989.

1988

109. Bahjat, Ahmad, *Ramadan Diary*, trans. Nirmeen A. Hassan. Cairo: GEBO.

110. Duwayri, Ra'fat, *Cat with Seven Lives*, trans. Carmen Weinstein and the author. Revised by M. M. Enani. Cairo: GEBO.

111. Elkhadem, Saad, *Avant-Garde Egyptian Fiction: The Ulysses Trilogy*, trans. Saad El-Gabalawy. Fredericton, NB, Canada: York Press.

112. Ghitani, Jamal. *Zayni Barakat*, trans. Farouk Mustafa [Abdel-Wahab]. London and New York: Penguin and Viking, 1988, 1990.

113. *Idris, Yusuf, *A Leader of Men*, trans. Saad Elkhadem. Fredericton, NB, Canada: York Press.

114. *Iraqi Short Stories: An Anthology*, ed. Yassen Taha Hafidh and Lutfiyah al-Dulaimi. Baghdad: Dar al-Mamun for Translation and Publication [Includes thirty-eight short stories representing pre- and post-1950 generations of Iraqi writers: Ghazi al-Abbadi, Khudayyir Abd al-Amir, Muhammad Abd al-Majid, Abd al-Ilah Abd al-Razzaq, Dayzi al-Amir, Saad al-Bazzaz, Ghanim al-Dabbagh, Mahmud al-Dahir,

Lutfiyyah al-Dulaymi, Maysalun Hadi, Muhammad Hayyawi, Mahmud Jindari, Adil Kamil, Ahmad Khalaf, Ja'far al-Khalili, Burhan al-Khatib, Muwaffaq Khidr, Muhammad Khudayyir, 'A'id Khusbak, Natiq Khulusi, Musa Kuraydi, Jihad Majid, Abd al-Razzaq al-Muttalibi, May Muzaffar, Abd al-Sattar Nasir, Abd al-Malik Nuri, Abd al-Khaliq al-Rikabi, Abd al-Majid al-Rubay'i, Adnan al-Rubay'i, Idmun Sabri, Nizar Salim, Suhaylah Salman, Warid Badr al-Salim, Mahdi 'Isa al-Saqr, Fu'ad Takarli, Amjad Tawfiq, Faraj Yasin and Najman Yasin]. (I)

115. *The Literature of Modern Arabia: An Anthology*, ed. Salma Khadra Jayyusi. London and New York: Kegan Paul International [Includes short stories and extracts of novels by more than thirty writers from the Arabian peninsula region: Muhammad Abd al-Malik, Mayfa' Abd al-Rahman, Muhammad Abd al-Wali, Abd al-Hamid Ahmad, Muhammad Alwan, Abd al-Qadir al-Aqil, Da'id al-Awlaqi, Salih Sa'id Ba Amr, Fawziyyah al-Bakr, Hamza Bogary, Zaid Muti' Dammaj, Khalil al-Fuzay', Muhammad Hasan Harbi, Kamal Haydar, Muhammad Salih Haydara, Mansur al-Hazimi, Husayn Ali Husayn, Isma'il Fahd Isma'il, Abd Allah Ali Khalifah, Muhammad al-Murr, Muhammad al-Muthanna, Ibrahim al-Nasir, Abd al-Majid al-Qadi, Walid al-Rujayb, Amin Salih, Abd Allah al-Salmi, Khayriyyah al-Saqqaf, Zayn al-Saqqaf, Muhammad Sa'id Sayf, Ali Sayyar, Ruqayyah al-Shabib, Sharifah Shamlan, Sulayman al-Shatti, Ahmad al-Siba'i, Layla Uthman and Siba'i Saqr al-Rushud]. (AW)

116. Mahfuz, Najib, *Fountain and Tomb*, trans. Soad Sobhi, Essam Fattouh and James Kennesson. Washington, DC: Three Continents Press.

117. *Modern Syrian Short Stories*, trans. Michel Azrak. Revised by M. J. L. Young. Washington: Three Continents Press [Includes stories by Abd al-Allah Abid, John Alexan, Haydar Haydar, Sa'id Huraniyyah, Ulfat Idlibi, Walid Ikhlasi, Kulit al-Khuri, Sabah Muhyi al-Din, Hani al-Rahib, Yasin Rifa'iyyah, George Salim, Ghadah al-Samman, Fu'ad al-Shayib, Fadil al-Siba'i, Nabil Sulayman, Muzaffar Sultan, Zakariya Tamir and Abd al-Salam al-'Ujayli]. (S)

118. Munif, Abdelrahman, *Endings*, trans. Roger Allen. London: Quartet Books. (J/SA)

119. *Sa'dani, Mahmud, *Black Sky and Other Stories*, trans. Nayla Nagib. Cairo: GEBO. Second English edition. The Black Heaven and Other Stories London: Kamel Graphics, 1991.

120. al-Sa'dawi, Nawal, *The Fall of the Imam*, trans. Sherif Hetata. London: Methuen; London: Saqi, 2001/2002.

121. —— *Memoirs of A Woman Doctor*, trans. Catherine Cobham. London: Saqi; San Francisco: City Lights Books, 1989; London: Saqi, 2000.

122. *Tubya, Majid, *Nine Short Stories*, trans. Nadia Gohar. Cairo: GEBO.

1989

123. *Abu Zayd, Layla, *Year of the Elephant: A Moroccan Woman's Journey toward Independence and Other Stories*, trans. Barbara Parmenter. Austin, TX: Center for Middle Eastern Studies, The University of Texas. (M)

124. Badr, Liyanah, *A Compass for the Sunflower*, trans. Catherine Cobham. London: The Women's Press. (P)

125. Elkhadem, Saad, *The Plague*, trans. Saad El-Gabalawy. Fredericton, NB, Canada: York Press.

126. Haykal, Muhammad Husayn, *Zainab*, trans. John Mohammed Grinsted. London: Darf.

127. Kharrat, Idwar, *City of Saffron*, trans. Frances Liardet. London: Quartet Books.

128. Khuri, Ilyas, *The Little Mountain*, trans. Maia Tabet. Minneapolis: University of Minnesota Press. (L)

129. *A Land of Stone and Thyme: Palestinian Short Stories*, ed. Abdelwahab and Nur Elmessiri. Winchester, MA: Faber and Faber; London: Quartet Books, 1996. (P)

130. Mahfuz, Najib, *The Day the Leader Was Killed*, trans. Malak Hashem. Cairo: GEBO, Cairo: AUCP, 1997; New York: Anchor Books, 2000.

131. —— *Midaq Alley, The Thief and the Dogs, Miramar* New York: Quality Paperback Book Club.

132. —— *Palace Walk*, trans. William M. Hutchins and Olive E. Kenny. Cairo: AUCP; New York: Doubleday, 1990. See also The Cairo Trilogy New York: Alfred A. Knopf, 2001; London: Everyman, 2001.

133. *The Modern Arabic Short Story: Shahrazad Returns, trans. Mohammad Shaheen. Basingstoke, UK: Macmillan Press [Includes Shaheen's translation of nine short stories or extracts from the works of Mustafa al-Masannawi. Mohammad Qindil, Zakariyya Tamir, Imile Habibi, Ibrahim al-Alam, Mahmud Shuqayr, Sa'd Makkawi, Akram Haniyyah and Natiq Khulusi, pp. 114–151]; New York: Palgrave Macmillan, 2002. (AW)

134. *Modern Egyptian Stories*, trans. Gamal Abd El-Nasser. Cairo: GEBO.

135. Qasim, Abd al-Hakim, *The Seven Days of Man*, trans. Joseph N. Bell. Cairo: GEBO; Evanston, IL: Northwestern University Press, 1996.

136. al-Sa'dawi, Nawal, *The Circling Song*, trans. Marilyn Booth. London: Zed Books.

137. al-Shaykh, Hanan, *Women of Sand and Myrrh*, trans. Catherine Cobham. London: Quartet Books, 1989, 1993; New York: Anchor Books, 1989, 1992. (L)

138. **Stories from the Rest of the World. The Graywolf Annual Six*, ed. Scott Walker. St Paul, MN: Graywolf Press. [Out of thirteen short stories included in this anthology, six are Arabic. Translated by Denys Johnson-Davies and originally published in *Arabic Short Stories* (1967) and *Modern Arab Short Stories* (1983), they are by Dhu'l Nun Ayyoub (Iraq), Ghassan Kanafani (Palestine), Mohammed Khudayyir (Iraq), Ibrahim al-Kuni (Libya), Alifa Rifaat (Egypt) and Zakaria Tamer (Syria)]. (AW)

1990

139. *Aslan, Ibrahim, *Evening Lake and Other Short Stories*, trans. Hoda El-Sadda. Cairo: GEBO.

140. *Assassination of Light: Modern Saudi Short Stories*, trans. Abu Bakr Bagader and Ava Molnar Heinrichsdorff. Washington, DC: Three Continents Press [Includes short stories by Ghalib Hamzah Abu al-Faraj, Fu'ad Anqawi, Hijab Yahya al-Hazimi, Ahmad Rida Huhu, Muhammad Ali al-Maghribi, Mahmud 'Isa al-Mashhadi, Muhammad al-Mulbari, Ibrahim al-Nasir, Muhammad Ali Rida Quddus, Amin Salim Ruwayhi, Khayriyyah al-Saqqaf, Sharifah al-Shamlan, Muhammad Ali al-Shaykh, Ahmad al-Subay'i, Hussah Muhammad al-Tuwayjiri and Luqman Yunus]. (SA)

141. Barakat, Halim, *Six Days*, trans. Bassam Frangieh and Scott McGehee. Washington, DC: Three Continents Press. (L)

142. Elkhadem, Saad, Canadian Adventures of the Flying Egyptian, trans. Saad El-Gabalawy. Fredericton, NB, Canada: York Press.

143. al-Hakim, Tawfiq, *Return of the Spirit*, trans. William M Hutchins. Washington, DC: Three Continents Press.

144. *Idris, Yusuf, *The Language of Pain*, trans. Nawal Naguib. Cairo: GEBO.

145. *Kanafani, Ghassan, *All That's Left to You: A Novella and Other Stories*, trans. May Jayyusi and Jeremy Reed. University of Texas at Austin: Center for Middle Eastern Studies; Cairo: AUCP. (P)

146. *Opening the Gates: A Century of Arab Feminist Writing*, ed. Margot Badran and Miriam Cooke. Bloomington, IN: Indiana University Press [Includes numerous short stories or extracts of novels by women writers from different Arab countries: Sufi Abd Allah, Dayzi al-Amir, Ihsan 'Assal, Samar Attar, Samirah Azzam, Fatima Mernissi, Emily Nasrallah, Nuha Radwan, Alifah Rif'at, Nawal Sa'dawi, Nuha Samarah, Khayriyyah Saqqaf and Hanan al-Shaykh]. (AW)

1991

147. Bogary, Hamza, *The Sheltered Quarter: A Tale of Boyhood in Mecca*, trans. Olive Kenny and Jeremy Reed. Austin: Center for Middle Eastern Studies, University of Texas. (SA)

148. *Du'aji, Ali, *Sleepless Nights*, trans. William Granara. Carthage/Tunis: Beit al-Hikma. (T)

149. *Gorgy [Jurji], Nabil Naoum, *The Slave's Dream and Other Stories*, trans. Denys Johnson-Davies. London: Quartet Books.

150. Ibrahim, Jamil Atiyah, *Down to the Sea*, trans. Frances Liardet. London: Quartet Books.

151. *Idris, Yusuf, *Selected Stories*, trans. Dalya Cohen-Mor. Exeter, UK: Ithaca.

152. *—— *Three Egyptian Short Stories*, trans. Saad El-Gabalawy. Fredericton, NB, Canada: York Press.

153. Mahfuz, Najib, *Palace of Desire: The Cairo Trilogy II*, trans. William M. Hutchins et al. Cairo: AUCP; New York: Doubleday, 1993, London: Black Swan, 1994. See also The Cairo Trilogy New York: Alfred A. Knopf, 2001.

154. *—— *The Time and the Place and Other Stories*, trans. Denys Johnson-Davies. New York: Doubleday; Cairo: AUCP; 2001.

155. Munif, Abdelrahman, *The Trench*, trans. Peter Theroux. New York: Pantheon Books, 1991; New York: Vintage Books, 1993. (J/SA)

156. *Murr, Muhammad, *Dubai Tales*, trans. Peter Clark. London/Boston, MA: Forest Books. (U)

157. al-Sa'dawi, Nawal, *Searching*, trans. Shirley Eber. London: Zed Books.

158. *Stories by Egyptian Women: My Grandmother's Cactus*, trans. Marilyn Booth. London: Quartet Books; Austin: University of Texas Press, 1993 [Includes stories by Radwa Ashur, Salwa Bakr, Siham Bayyumi, Ni'mat al-Buhayri, I'tidal Uthman, Muna Rajab, Ibtihal Salim and Sahar Tawfiq].

159. Zangana, Haifa, *Through the Vast Halls of Memory*, trans. Paul Hammond and the author. Paris: Hourglass. (I)

1992

160. Abaza, Tharwat, *A Touch of Fear*, trans. Rafik Basil. Cairo: GEBO.

161. *An Anthology of Modern Palestinian Literature*, ed. Salma Khadra Jayyusi. New York: Columbia University Press [Includes short stories, extracts of novels and autobiographical accounts by more than thirty Palestinian writers: Ibrahim al-'Absi, Salih Abu Usba', Gharib Asqalani, Samirah Azzam, Liyanah Badr, Riyad Baydas, Zaki Darwish, Najwa Qa'war Farah, Tawfiq Fayyad, Emile Habibi, Akram Haniyyah, Mahmud Say al-Din al-Irani, Ghassan Kanafani, Sahar Khalifah, Muhammad Naffa', Walid Rabah, Yahya Rabah, Fadl al-Rimawi, Mahmud al-Rimawi, Khalil al-Sawahiri, Mahmud Shahin, Sulayman al-Shaykh, Yusuf Shururu, Mahmud Shuqayr, Muhammad Ali Taha, Faruq Wadi and Yahya Yakhlif]. (P)

162. Badr, Liyanah, *A Balcony over the Fakihani: Three Novellas* ['A Land of Rock and Thyme', 'A Balcony over the Fakihani' and 'Canary and the Sea'], trans. Peter Clark with Christopher Tingley. New York: Interlink Books; Interlink Books, 2002. (P)

163. *Bakr, Salwa, *Such a Beautiful Voice*, trans. Hoda el-Sadda. Cairo: GEBO; New Delhi: Kali for Women, 1994.

164. *—— *The Wiles of Men and Other Stories*, trans. Denys Johnson-Davies. London: Quartet Books; Austin, TX: University of Texas Press, 1993.

165. Fayyad, Sulayman, *Voices*, trans. Hosam Aboul Ela. New York: Marion Boyars Publishers, 1992/1993.

166. *al-Hamamisi, Abd al-'Al, *Short Stories*, trans. Hala El-Borollosy. Revised by M. M. Enani. Cairo: GEBO.

167. Ibyari, Fathi, *A Journey outside the Game*, trans. Nadia El-Kholi. Cairo: GEBO.

168. *Idris, Yusuf, *Short Stories. Selections. The Piper Dies and Other Stories*, trans. Dalya Cohen-Mor. Potomac, MD: Sheba Press.

169. *Maghreb: New Writing from North Africa*, ed. Jacqueline Kaye. York, UK: Talus Editions, University of York [Includes short stories by Abdeljabbar Essehimi, Ahmad al-Madini and Muhammad Zafzaf, and an extract from Abdallah Laroui's novel *Awraq*]. (M)

170. *Mahfuz, Najib, *Egyptian Time*, trans. Peter Theroux. Photographs by Robert Lyons. New York: Doubleday.

171. —— *The Journey of Ibn Fattouma*, trans. Denys Johnson-Davies. New York: Doubleday.

172. —— *Sugar Street*, trans. William M. Hutchins and Angele Botros Samaan. Cairo: AUCP; New York: Doubleday, London: Black Swan, 1994. See also The Cairo Trilogy New York: Alfred A. Knopf, 2001.

173. al-Muwaylihi, Muhammad and Roger Allen, *A Period of Time*. Reading, UK: Ithaca [Part One: A Study of Muhammad al-Muwaylihi's Hadith Isa ibn Hisham by Roger Allen. Part Two: A translation of the third edition of Muhammad al-Muwaylihi's Hadith Isa ibn Hisham by Roger Allen. Previous edition: published in microfiche as *A Study of Haith Isa ibn Hisham*. New York: State University of New York, p. 1074].

174. *Nasrallah, Emily, *A House Not her Own: Stories from Beirut*, trans. Thoraya Khalil-Khouri. Charlottetown, PEI, Canada: Gynergy Books. (L)

1993

175. *An Arabian Mosaic: Short Stories by Arab Women Writers*, trans. Dalya Cohen-Mor. Potomac, MD: Sheba Press [Includes stories by Sufi Abd Allah, Daisy al-Amir, Samirah Azzam, Layla Ba'labakki, Layla Bin Mami, Zaynab Fahmi, Sakinah Fu'ad, Ulfa Idlibi, Ihsan Kamal, Kulit Suhayl al-Khuri, Nawal al-Sa'dawi, Ghadad al-Samman, Khayriyyah al-Saqqaf, Sharifah al-Shamlan, Hanan al-Shaykh, Layla al-Uthman, Latifah al-Zayyat, May Ziyadah]. (AW)

176. *Husayn, Taha, *The Sufferers: Stories and Polemics*, trans. Mona El-Zayyat. Cairo: AUCP.

177. Kharrat, Idwar, *Girls of Alexandria*, trans. Frances Liardet. London: Quartet Books.

178. Khuri, Ilyas, *Gates of the City*, trans. Paula Haydar. Minneapolis: University of Minnesota Press. (L)

179. Mahfuz, Najib, *Adrift on the Nile*, trans. Jean Liardet. Cairo: AUCP; New York: Anchor Books; Cairo: AUCP, 2001; Stuart, FL: Braille International, 2002.

180. —— *The Harafish*, trans. Catherine Cobham. New York: Doubleday.

181. Minah, Hanna, *Fragments of Memory: A Story of A Syrian Family*, trans. Olive Kenny and Lorne Kenny. Austin, TX: Center for Middle Eastern Studies, The University of Texas. (S)

182. * *Modern Jordanian Fiction: A Selection*, trans. Fahd Salameh. Amman: Ministry of Culture [Includes comments and translated sections]. (J)

183. Munif, Abdelrahman, *Variations on Night and Day*, trans. Peter Theroux. New York: Pantheon Books; New York: Vintage Books, 1994. (J/SA)

184. Nasr Allah, Ibrahim, *Prairies of Fever*, trans. May Jayyusi and Jeremy Reed. New York: Interlink Books. (P)

185. *Passport to Arabia*, ed. Mike Gerrard and Thomas McCarthy. Wistow, Huntingdon: Passport; London: Serpent's Tail [Includes mostly reprinted short stories by Liyanah Badr, Jabra I. Jabra, Ibrahim al-Kuni, Najib Mahfuz, Emily Nasrallah, Sara al-Nawwaf (*nom-de-plume* of an UAE writer), Nawal al-Sa'dawi, and Muhammad Salamawi]. (AW)

186. al-Sa'dawi, Nawal, *The Well of Life; and The Thread*, trans. Sharif Hetata. London: Lime Tree.

187. *Taymur, Mahmud, *Sensuous Lips and Other Stories*, trans. Nayla Naguib. Cairo: GEBO.

1994

188. *al-Amir, Dayzi, *The Waiting List: An Iraqi Woman's Tales of Alienation*, trans. Barbara Parmenter. Austin, TX: Center for Middle Eastern Studies, University of Texas. (I)

189. Attar, Samar, *Lina: Portrait of a Damascene Girl* Colorado Springs, CO: Three Continents Press. (S)

190. Badr, Liyanah, *The Eye of the Mirror*, trans. Samira Kawar. Reading: Garnet. (P)

191. Barakat, Huda, *The Stone of Laughter*, trans. Sophie Bennett. Reading: Garnet. (P)

192. *Bisati, Muhammad, *A Last Glass of Tea and Other Stories*, trans. Denys Johnson-Davies. Cairo: AUCP; Washington, DC: Three Continents Press, 1995; Boulder, CO: Lynne Rienner, 1998.

193. **Blood into Ink: South Asian and Middle Eastern Women Write War*, ed. Miriam Cooke and Roshni Rustomji-Kerns. Boulder, CO: Westview Press, 1994. [Includes short stories and extracts of novels by Dayzi al-Amir, Samirah Azzam, Sahar Khalifah, Emily Nasrallah, Nuha Samara, Ghadah Samman, Aliya Shuaib and Aliya Talib]. (AW)

194. Dammaj, Zayd Muti', *The Hostage*, trans. May Jayyusi and Christopher Tingley. New York: Interlink Books. (Y)

195. *Elkhadem, Saad, *Five Innovative Egyptian Short Stories*. Fredericton, NB, Canada: York Press.

196. —— *The Wings of Lead: A Modern Egyptian Novella* Fredericton, NB, Canada: York P.

197. *Ghanim, Fathi, *The Right Man and Other Stories*, trans. Nayla Naguib. Cairo: GEBO.

198. **Global Cultures: A Transnational Short Fiction Reader*, ed. Elizabeth Young-Bruehl. Hanover, NH: Wesleyan University Press [Includes reprinted short stories by Abd al-'Al al-Hamamisi, Ulfat Idlibi, Ghassan Kanafani, Alifa Rifaat and Abd al-Salam al-'Ujayli]. (AW)

199. Husayn, Taha, *A Man of Letters*, trans. Mona El-Zayyat. Cairo: AUCP.

200. Khuri, Ilyas, *The Journey of Little Gandhi*, trans. Paula Haydar. Minneapolis, MN: University of Minnesota Press. (L)

201. *Murr, Muhammad, *The Wink of Mona Lisa and Other Stories from the Gulf*, trans. Jack Briggs. Dubai, UAE: Motivate Publishing. (U)

202. *Nasrallah, Emily, *The Fantastic Strokes of Imagination*, trans. Rebecca Porteous. Cairo: Elias Modern Publishing House. (L)

203. Sab'awi [Sabawi], Abd al-Karim, *The Phoenix* [A translation of his novel *al-'Anqa'*]. Upper Ferntree Gully, Victoria, Australia: Papyrus Publishing House.(P)

204. *al-Shaykh, Hanan, *I Sweep the Sun off Rooftops*. A collection of twelve short stories translated by Denys Johnson-Davies and others. St Leonards, Australia: Allen & Unwin. (L)

205. Turjuman, Siham, *Daughter of Damascus*, trans. Andrea Rugh. Austin: University of Texas Press. (S)

206. *A Voice of their Own: Short Stories by Egyptian Women*, ed. and intro. Angele Botros Samaan. Giza/Cairo: Foreign Cultural Information Department, Prism Literary Series.

1995

207. **An Anthology of Moroccan Short Stories*, trans. Malcolm Williams and Gavin Watterson. Tangier: King Fahd's School of Translation, Abdelmalek Essaadi University. (M)

208. Bakr, Salwa, *The Golden Chariot*, trans. Dinah Manisty. Reading, UK: Garnet.

209. Faqih, Ahmad Ibrahim, *Gardens of the Night: A Trilogy*, trans. Russell Harris, Amin al-'Ayouti and Suraya 'Allam. London: Quartet Books. (LI)

210. ***Global Voices: Contemporary Literature from the Non-Western World*, ed. Arthur W. Biddle, Gloria Bien et al. Englewood Cliffs, NJ: Prentice Hall. [Includes reprinted stories by Layla Baalbaki, 'A Spaceship of Tenderness to the Moon'; Ghassan Kanafani, 'Death of Bed Number 12'; Najib Mahfuz 'Zaabalawi'; Emily Nasrallah 'Our Daily Bread'; and Tayeb Salih 'The Doum Tree of Wad Hamid']. (AW)

211. *al-Hakim, Tawfiq, *Metaphysical Tales: Selected Short Stories*, trans. William M. Hutchins. Colorado Springs, CO: Three Continents Press.

212. Idlibi, Ulfat, *Sabriya: Damascus Bitter Sweet*, trans. Peter Clark. London: Quartet Books. (S)

213. *Mahfuz, Najib, *Arabian Nights and Days*, trans. Denys Johnson-Davies. New York: Doubleday.

214. ***Modern Literature of the Non-Western World: Where the Rivers Are Born*. Ed. Jayana Clerk and Ruth Siegel. New York: HarperCollins [Includes reprinted short stories by Abd al-Hamid Ahmad (UAE), Sa'id Aulaqi (Yemen), Yahya Haqqi and Yusuf Idris (Egypt), Ghassan Kanafani (Palestine), Muhammad Khudayyir (Iraq), Najib Mahfuz and Nawal al-Sa'dawi (Egypt)]. (AW)

215. Musa, Sabri, *Seeds of Corruption*, trans. Elizabeth Moussa. Cairo: GEBO.

216. Na'na', Hamidah, *The Homeland*, trans. Martin Asser. Reading, UK: Garnet. (P)

217. Qasim, Abd al-Hakim, *Rites of Assent*, trans. Peter Theroux. Philadelphia, PA: Temple University Press.

218. al-Sa'dawi, Nawal, *The Innocence of the Devil*, trans. Sherif Hetata. London: Methuen; Berkeley: University of California Press, 1994.

219. Samman, Ghadah, *Beirut '75*, trans. Nancy N. Roberts. Fayetteville, AR: University of Arkansas Press. (S)

220. al-Shaykh, Hanan, *Beirut Blues: A Novel*, trans. Catherine Cobham. New York: Anchor Books. (L)

221. Tawfiq, Sahar, *Points of the Compass*, trans. Marilyn Booth. Fayetteville, AR: University of Arkansas Press.

222. *Tubya, Majid, *The Emigration to the North Country of Hathoot's Tribe*, trans. Wadida Wassef. Cairo: GEBO.

1996

223. Baradah, Muhammad, *The Game of Forgetting*, trans. Issa Boullata. Austin, TX: Center for Middle Eastern Studies, The University of Texas; London: Quartet Books, 1997. (M)

224. Khuri, Ilyas, *The Kingdom of Strangers*, trans. Paula Haydar. Fayetteville, AR: University of Arkansas Press. (L)

225. Mahfuz, Najib, *Children of the Alley*, trans. Peter Theroux. New York: Doubleday.

226. Mamduh, Aliyah, *Mothballs*, trans. Peter Theroux. Reading, UK: Garnet. (I)

227. al-Qusaybi, Ghazi Abd al-Rahman, *An Apartment Called Freedom*, trans. Leslie McLoughlin. London: Kegan Paul International. (SA)

228. Salih, Tayeb, *Bandarshah*, trans. Denys Johnson-Davies. London and New York: Kegan Paul. (SU)

229. *A Selection of Jordanian Short Stories*, trans. Abd Allah Shunnaq and Nancy Roberts. Irbid, Jordan: Dar al-Hilal for Translation. (J)

230. * Sharuni, Yusuf, *The Five Lovers*, trans. unknown. Cairo: GEBO.

231. al-Shaykh, Hanan, *Beirut Blues*, trans. Catherine Cobham. New York: Anchor Books; London: Vintage, 1996. (L)

232. *Short Fiction by Saudi Women Writers*, trans. Aman Mahmoud Attieh. Colorado Springs, CO: Three Continents Press; Austin, TX:

Department of Middle Eastern Languages and Cultures, University of Texas, 1999. (SA)

233. Shukri, Muhammad, Streetwise, trans. Ed Emery. London: Saqi, 1996, 2000. (M)

234. Tahir, Baha', *Aunt Safiyya and the Monastery*, trans. Barbara Romaine. Berkeley: University of California Press.

235. **Writing through Literature, ed. Linda Anstendig and David Hicks. Englewood Cliffs, NJ: Prentice Hall [Includes Najib Mahfouz's 'Half A Day' trans. by Denys Johnson-Davies].

1997

236. Abd al-Majid, Ibrahim [also known as Abdel Meguid], *The Other Place*, trans. Farouk Abdel Wahab. Cairo: AUCP.

237. Bisati, Muhammad, *Houses behind the Trees*, trans. Denys Johnson-Davies. Cairo: AUCP.

238. Ghitani, Jamal, *A Distress Call*, trans. Soad Naguib. Revised by M. M. Enani. Cairo: GEBO.

239. Husayn, Taha, *The Tree of Misery*, trans. Mona El-Zayyat. Cairo: Palm Press.

240. Minah, Hanna, *Sun on a Cloudy Day*, trans. Bassam Frangieh and Clementina Brown. Pueblo, CO: Passeggiata Press. (S)

241. al-Qa'id, Muhammad Yusuf, *The Days of Drought*, trans. George Takla. Cairo: GEBO.

242. Rizq, Abd al-Fattah, *Stark Naked*, trans. Soad Mahmoud Naguib. Revised by M. M. Enani. Cairo: GEBO.

243. Samman, Ghadah, *Beirut Nightmares*, trans. Nancy N. Roberts. London: Quartet Books.

244. Wadi, Taha 'Imran, *The Distant Horizon*, trans. Hala al-Borollosy; Ed. Hilary Press. Cairo: GEBO.

245. Yarid, Nazik Saba, *Improvisations on a Missing String*, trans. Stuart A. Hancox. Fayetteville, AR: University of Arkansas Press. (L)

246. Zayyat, Latifah, *The Owner of the House*, trans. Sophie Bennett. London: Quartet Books.

1998

247. Ali, Idris, *Dongola: A Novel of Nubia*, trans. Peter Theroux. Fayetteville, AR: University of Arkansas Press.

248. Attar, Samar, *The House on 'Arnus Square* Pueblo, CO: Passeggiata Press. (S)

249. Bal'id, Mahmud, *When the Drums Beat: A Collection of Tunisian Short Stories*, trans. Abd Allah Shunnaq and Muhammed Farghal. Irbid, Jordan: Dar al-Hilal. (T)

250. Elkhadem, Saad, *Two Avant-Garde Egyptian Novels; From Travels of the Egyptian Odysseus* Toronto: York Press.

251. *al-Hakim, Tawfiq, *In the Tavern of Life and Other Stories*, trans. William M. Hutchins. Boulder, CO: Lynne Rienner.

252. Idlibi, Ulfat, Grandfather's Tale, trans. Peter Clark. London: Quartet Books. (S)

253. Jalal, Muhammad, *Mawardi Café*, trans. Marlyn Iskandar. Revised by Mursi Saad Eddin. Cairo: GEBO.

254. *Jawhar, Yusuf, *The Blind Lamp-Post and Other Stories*, trans. Nayla Naguib. Cairo: GEBO.

255. Jubril, Muhammad, *The Other Shore*, trans. Gamel Abdel Nasser. Revised by M. M. Enani. Cairo: GEBO.

256. *Kafrawi, Sa'id, *The Hill of Gypsies and Other Stories*, trans. Denys Johnson-Davies. Cairo: AUCP.

257. Mahfuz, Najib, *Akhenaten, Dweller in Truth*, trans. Tagreid Abu Hassabo. Cairo: AUCP; New York: Anchor Books, 2000.

258. *Modern Palestinian Short Stories in Translation, ed. Izzat Ghazzawi and Claire Peak. Jerusalem: The Palestinian Writers' Union, 1998 [Published under the auspices of the Norwegian Authors' Union, this anthology presents short stories of forty-four Palestinian writers, most of whom were born after 1948. The stories reflect the ordeal of the Palestinians as they struggle to regain their rights and pursue their search 'for freedom in its wide political, social, and existential sense']. (P)

259. *A Sad Tune on a Spanish Fiddle and Other Jordanian Short Stories*, trans. Abd Allah Shunnaq. Irbid, Jordan: Dar al-Hilal. (J)

260. Samman, Ghadah, *The Square Moon: Supernatural Tales*, trans. Issa J. Boullata. Fayetteville, AR: University of Arkansas Press. (S)

261. Tahawi, Miral. *The Tent*, trans. Anthony Calderbank. Cairo: AUCP.

262. *Wadi, Taha 'Imran, *Desire and Thirst: Egyptian Short Stories*, trans. Abd al-Mun'im Ali. Revised by Hilda Spear. Cairo: GEBO.

263. **A Web of Stories: An Introduction to Short Fiction, ed. Jon Ford and Marjorie Ford. Englewood Cliffs, NJ: Prentice Hall [Najib Mahfuz's 'The Norwegian Rat'].

1999

264. Abd al-Majid, Ibrahim, *No One Sleeps in Alexandria*, trans. Farouk Abdel Wahab. Cairo: AUCP.

265. Da'if, Rashid, *Dear Mr Kawabata*, trans. Paul Starkey. London: Quartet Books. (L)

266. Daoud, Hassan, *The House of Mathilde*, trans. Peter Theroux. London: Granta Books. (L)

267. *The Echo of Kuwaiti Creativity: A Collection of Translated Short Stories*, trans. Haifa al-Sanousi. Kuwait: Centre for Research and Studies on Kuwait. (K)

268. **Expanding Horizons: An Introduction of Non-Western Humanities, ed. Janice C. Buchanan and Patricia J. Chauvin. Englewood Cliffs, NJ: Prentice Hall [Includes Najib Mahfuz's ' Excerpt from Sugar Street', in addition to Fatima Mernissi].

269. Haqqi, Yahya, *Blood and Mud: Three Novelettes* [*The Posmaster, Abu Foda* and *The Gypsy*], trans. Pierre Cachia. Pueblo, CO: Passeggiata Press.

270. al-Husayni, Ishaq Musa, *Memoirs of a Hen: A Present-Day Palestinian Fable*, trans. Jurj Qanazi [George J. Kanazi]. Toronto, Ont.: York Press. (P)

271. Idris, Yusuf, *City of Love and Ashes*, trans. R. Neil Hewison. Cairo: AUCP; 2002.

272. **Literatures of Asia, Africa, and Latin America*, ed. Willis Barnstone and Tony Barnstone. Upper Saddle River, NJ: Prentice Hall [Includes stories by Muhammad Bisati, Haydar Haydar, Yusuf Idris, Najib Mahfuz and Nawal al-Sa'dawi]. (AW)

273. * Short Stories by Saudi Arabian Women Writers, trans. Abubaker Bagader, Ava M. Heinrichsdorff, Deborah S. Akers; additional translations by Abdul-Aziz al- Sebail. Boulder, CO: Lynne Rienner [Includes stories by Amal Abd al-Hamid, Raja' 'Alim, Lamya' Ba

Ashin, Badriyah al-Bishr, Sarah Bu Haymad, Fatimah al-Dawsari, Muna al-Dhukayr, Jamilah Fatani, Nurah al-Ghamidi, Samirah Khashuqji, Najat Khayyat, Wafa' Munawwar, Khayriyyah al-Saqqaf, Sharifah al-Shamlan, Qumashah al-'Ulayyan, Fatimah al-'Utaybi]. (SA)

274. **The World of Literature, ed. Louis Westling et al. Englewood Cliffs, NJ: Prentice Hall [Includes Najib Mahfuz and Salwa Bakr].

275. Yakhlif, Yahya, *A Lake beyond the Wind*, trans. May Jayyusi and Christopher Tingley. New York: Interlink Books. (P)

2000

276. Abu Zayd, Layla, The Last Chapter, trans. John Liechy and the author. Cairo: AUCP. (M)

277. *Faqih, Ahmad Ibrahim, *Who's Afraid of Agatha Christie? and Other Short Stories* London: Kegan Paul. (LI)

278. *——— *Charles, Diana, and Me and Other Stories* London: Kegan Paul. (LI)

279. *——— *Valley of Ashes* London: Kegan Paul. (LI)

280. Jabra, Jabra I., *In Search of Walid Masoud*, trans. Roger Allen and Adnan Haydar. Syracuse, NY: Syracuse University Press. (P)

281. * Kanafani, Ghassan, *Palestine's Children: Returning to Haifa and Other Stories*, trans. Barbara Harlow and Karen Riley. Boulder, CO: Lynne Rienner. (P)

282. *Libyan Stories: Twelve Short Stories from Libya*, ed. Ahmad Ibrahim Faqih. London, New York: Kegan Paul International [Includes stories by Ibrahim al- Faqih, Bashir al-Hashimi, Ibrahim al-Kuni, Ali al-Misrati, K. H. Mustafa, Abd Allah al-Quayri, Yusuf al-Quwayri, Yusuf al-Sharif, Kamil al-Maghor, Khalifa Takbali, Sayed Gaddaf-Addam and M. al-Shwihdi]. (LI)

283. Mahfuz, Najib, *The Beggar; The Thief and the Dogs; Autumn Quail* New York: Anchor Books.

284. Mosteghanemi, Ahlem [Mustaghanimi, Ahlam], Memory in Flesh, trans. Baria Ahmar Sreih. Cairo: AUCP; 2003. (A)

285. *Short Story in the UAE, ed. M. Daoud Tahboub. UAE: Ministry of Information and Culture [Includes fourteen short stories]. (U)

286. Telmissany, May [Tilimsani, Mayy], Dunyazad, trans. Roger Allen. London: Saqi.

287. **Under the Naked Sky: Short Stories from the Arab World*, trans. Denys Johnson-Davies. Cairo: AUCP; 2003; London: Saqi, 2001 [Includes short stories by Yusuf Abu Rayya, Ibrahim Aslan, Hana Atiyyah, Abdullah Bakhshawin, Salwa Bakr, Mohammad Bisati, Ibrahim Dargouthi, Jamal Ghitani, Ghalib Halasa, Yusuf Idris, Abduh Jubayr, In'am Kachachi, Sa'id Kafrawi, Idwar Kharrat, Muhammad Khudayyir, Ibrahim Kuni, Najib Mahfuz, Muhammad Makhzanji, Aliya Mamduh, Abd al-Aziz Mishri, Buthaynah al-Nasiri, Ibrahim Samau'il, Salma Matar Sayf, Khayri Shalabi, Hanan al-Shaykh, Fu'ad Takarli, Zakariya Tamir, Mahmud Wardani, Muhammad Zafzaf, Amina Zaydan]. (AW)

288. Wattar, al-Tahir, *The Earthquake*, trans. William Granara. London: Saqi. (A)

289. Zayyat, Latifah, *The Open Door*, trans. Marilyn Booth. Cairo: AUCP.

2001

290. Abd al-Wali, Muhammad, *They Die Strangers*, trans. Abubaker Bagader and Deborah Akers. Austin, TX: Center for Middle Eastern Studies, University of Texas. (Y)

291. Barakat, Huda, *The Tiller of Waters*, trans. Marilyn Booth. Cairo: AUCP. (L)

292. Da'if, Rashid, *Passage to Dusk*, trans. Nirvana Tanoukhi. Austin, TX: Center for Middle Eastern Studies, University of Texas. (L)

293. —— *This Side of Innocence*, trans. Paula Haydar. New York; Northampton: Interlink Books. (L)

294. Duwayhi, Jabbur, *Autumn Equinox*, trans. Nay Hannawi. Fayetteville, AR: University of Arkansas Press. (L)

295. Elkhadem, Saad, *One Night in Cairo: An Egyptian Micronovel with Footnotes* Toronto: York Press.

296. Ibrahim, Sun'Allah, *Zaat*, trans. Anthony Calderbank. Cairo: AUCP.

297. Khedairi, Betool, *A Sky So Close*, trans. Muhayman Jamil. New York: Pantheon. (I)

298. Mahfuz, Najib, *Respected Sir; Wedding Song; The Search* New York: Anchor Books.

299. al-Sa'dawi, Nawal, *Love in the Kingdom of Oil*, trans. Basil Hatim and Malcolm Williams. London: Saqi.

300. al-Takarli, Fu'ad, *The Long Way Back*, trans. Catherine Cobham. Cairo: AUCP. (I)

2002

301. al-Atrash, Layla, *A Woman of Five Seasons*, trans. Nura Nuwayhid Halwani and Christopher Tingley. New York: Interlink Books. (P)

302. Baradah, Muhammad, *Fugitive Light*, trans. Issa J. Boullata. Syracuse, NY: Syracuse University Press. (M)

303. Ibrahim, Sun'Allah, *The Committee*, trans. May S. St. Germain and Charlene Constable. Cairo: AUCP.

304. Kharrat, Idwar, *Rama and the Dragon*, trans. Ferial Ghazoul and John Verlenden. Cairo: AUCP.

305. al-Kuni, Ibrahim, *The Bleeding of the Stone*, trans. May Jayyusi and Christopher Tingley. New York: Interlink Books. (LI)

306. *Mahfuz, Najib, *Voices from the Other World: Ancient Egyptian Tales*, trans. Raymond Stock. Cairo: AUCP.

307. *al-Nasiri, Buthaynah, *Final Night: Short Stories*, trans. Denys Johnson-Davies. Cairo: AUCP. (I)

308. al-Qusaybi, Ghazi, *A Love Story*, trans. Robin Bray. London: Saqi. (SA)

309. *Rajab, Muna, *Short Stories*, trans. M. Enani and A. Gafari. Cairo: GEBO.

310. Ramadan, Sumayyah, *Leaves of Narcissus*, trans. Marilyn Booth. Cairo: AUCP.

311. *Salim, Ibtihal, *Children of the Waters*, trans. Marilyn Booth. Austin, TX: Center for Middle Eastern Studies, The University of Texas.

312. Tahir, Baha', *Love in Exile*, trans. Farouk Abdel Wahab. Cairo: AUCP.

313. Tahawi, Miral, *Blue Aubergine*, trans. Anthony Calderbank. Cairo: AUCP.

314. al-Tukhi, Abd Allah, *The River: A Tetralogy* Part One, trans. Yussreya Abou-Hadid. Cairo: GEBO.

2003[1]

315. Ashur, Radwa, *Granada*, trans. William Granara. Syracuse, NY: Syracuse University Press.

316. Hamad, Turki, *Adama*, trans. Robin Bray. London: Saqi; St Paul, MN: Ruminator Books.

317. Khatib, Muhammad Kamil, *Just Like a River*, trans. Maher Barakat and Michelle Hartman. New York: Interlink Books. (S)

318. Mahfuz, Najib, *Thebes at War*, trans. Humphrey Davies. Cairo: AUCP.

319. —— *Khufu's Wisdom*, trans. Raymond Stock. Cairo: AUCP.

320. —— *Rhadopis of Nubia*, trans. Anthony Calderbank. Cairo: AUCP.

321. *Nasir, Abd Allah Muhammad, *The Tree and Other Stories*, trans. Dina Bosio and Christopher Tingley. New York: Interlink Books. (SA)

322. al-Ramli, Muhsin, *Scattered Crumbs*, trans. Yasmeen Hantoosh. Fayetteville, AR: University of Arkansas Press. (I)

Arabic Works in International Anthologies

**Afro–Asian Short Stories: An Anthology* Cairo: Permanent Bureau of Afro–Asian Writers. 2 vols [Vol. I includes stories from Algeria, Egypt, Morocco, Syria, Tunisia and Yemen. Vol. II has stories from Egypt, Iraq, Palestine and Sudan]. (AW)

**Stories from the Rest of the World. The Graywolf Annual Six*, ed. Scott Walker. St Paul, MN: Graywolf Press, 1989 [Out of thirteen short stories included in this anthology, six are Arabic. Translated by Denys Johnson-Davies and originally published in *Arabic Short Stories* (1967) and *Modern Arab Short Stories* (1983), they are by Dhu'l Nun Ayyoub, Ghassan Kanafani, Mohammed Khudayyir, Ibrahim al-Kuni, Alifa Rifaat and Zakaria Tamer]. (AW)

**Blood into Ink: South Asian and Middle Eastern Women Write War*, ed. Miriam Cooke and Roshni Rustomji-Kerns. Boulder, CO: Westview Press, 1994 [Includes short stories and extracts of novels by Dayzi al-Amir, Samirah

---

1. According to WorldCat, an English translation of Ilyas Khuri's *Gate to the Sun* was published in 2003. New York: Seven Stories; London: Turnaround, but the publisher's information indicated that it was still in press as late as April 2004.

Azzam, Sahar Khalifah, Emily Nasrallah, Nuha Samara, Ghadah Samman, Aliya Shuaib and Aliya Talib]. (AW)

**Global Cultures: A Transnational Short Fiction Reader*, ed. Elizabeth Young-Bruehl. Hanover, NH: Wesleyan University Press, 1994 [Includes reprinted short stories by Abd al-'Al al-Hamamisi, Ulfat Idlibi, Ghassan Kanafani, Alifa Rifaat and Abd al-Salam al-'Ujayli]. (AW)

**Global Voices: Contemporary Literature from the Non-Western World*, ed. Arthur W. Biddle, Gloria Bien et al. Englewood Cliffs, NJ: Prentice Hall, 1995 [Includes reprinted stories by Layla Baalbaki, 'A Spaceship of Tenderness to the Moon', Ghassan Kanafani, 'Death of Bed Number 12', Najib Mahfuz, 'Zaabalawi', Emily Nasrallah, 'Our Daily Bread' and Tayeb Salih, 'The Doum Tree of Wad Hamid']. (AW)

**Modern Literature of the Non-Western World: Where the Rivers Are Born*, ed. Jayana Clerk and Ruth Siegel. New York: HarperCollins, 1995 [Includes reprinted short stories by Abd al-Hamid Ahmad (UAE), Sa'id Aulaqi (Yemen), Yahya Haqqi and Yusuf Idris (Egypt), Ghassan Kanafani (Palestine), Muhammad Khudayyir (Iraq), Najib Mahfuz and Nawal al-Sa'dawi (Egypt)]. (AW)

**Writing through Literature*, ed. Linda Anstendig and David Hicks. Englewood Cliffs, NJ: Prentice Hall [Includes Najib Mahfouz's 'Half A Day' trans. by Denys Johnson-Davies].

**A Web of Stories: An Introduction to Short Fiction*, ed. Jon Ford and Marjorie Ford. Englewood Cliffs, NJ: Prentice Hall, 1998 [Najib Mahfuz's 'The Norwegian Rat'].

**Expanding Horizons: An Introduction to Non-Western Humanities*, ed. Janice C. Buchanan and Patricia J. Chauvin. Englewood Cliffs, NJ: Prentice Hall, 1999 [Includes Najib Mahfuz, ' Excerpt from Sugar Street', in addition to Fatima Mernissi].

**Literatures of Asia, Africa, and Latin America*, ed. Willis Barnstone and Tony Barnstone. Upper Saddle River, NJ: Prentice Hall, 1999 [Includes stories by Muhammad Bisati, Haydar Haydar, Yusuf Idris, Najib Mahfuz and Nawal al-Sa'dawi]. (AW)

**The World of Literature*, ed. Louis Westling et al. Englewood Cliffs, NJ: Prentice Hall, 1999 [Includes Najib Mahfuz and Salwa Bakr].

Authors Index

Abaza, Tharwat 160

Abd Allah, Muhammad Abd al-Halim 28

Abd Allah, Yahya Taher 71

Abd al-Majid, Ibrahim 236, 264

Abd al-Qaddus, Ihsan 40

Abd al-Wali, Muhammad 290

Abu Zayd, Layla 123, 276

Abushesha, Redwan 35

Ali, Idris 247

al-Amir, Daisy 188

al-'Aqqad, 'Abbas Mahmud 41

Ashur, Radwa 315

Aslan, Ibrahim 139

Atrash, Layla 301

Attar, Samar 189, 248

Awwad, Tawfiq 32

Badr, Liyanah 124, 162, 190

Bahjat, Ahmad 109

Bakr, Salwa 163, 164, 208

Bal'id, Mahmud 249

Baradah, Muhammad 223, 302

Barakat, Halim 29, 141

Barakat, Huda 191, 291

Bindari, Sami 53

Bisati, Muhammad 192, 237

Bogary, Hamza 147

Da'if, Rashid 265, 292, 293

Damanhuri, Hamid 11

Dammaj, Zayd Muti' 194

Daoud, Hassan 266

Du'aji, Ali 148

Duwayhi, Jabbur 294

Duwayri, Ra'fat 110

Elkhadem, Saad 48, 87, 111, 125, 142, 195, 196, 250, 295

Fahmi, Abdul Rahman 99

Faqih, Ahmad Ibrahim 209, 277, 278, 279

Fayyad, Sulayman 165

Ghanim, Fathi 12, 197

Ghitani, Jamal 88, 112, 238

Gorgy [Jurji], Nabil Naoum 149

Habibi, Emile 62

al-Hakim, Tawfiq 1, 13, 143, 211, 251

Hamad, Turki 316

Hamamisi, Abd al-'Al 166

Haqqi, Mahmud Tahir 89

Haqqi, Yahya 24, 100, 269

Haykal, Muhammad Husayn 126

Hetata, Sherif 63, 90

Husayn, Muhammad Kamil 6

Husayn, Taha 3, 30, 33, 54, 176, 199, 239

al-Husayni, Ishaq Musa 270

Ibrahim, Jamil Atiyah 150

Ibrahim, Sun'Allah 20, 296, 303

Ibyari, Fathi 167

Idlibi, Ulfat 212, 252

Idris, Yusuf 43, 44, 72, 73, 113, 144, 151, 152, 168, 271

Jabra, Jabra Ibrahim 80, 280

Jalal, Muhammad 91, 253

Jawhar, Yusuf 254

Jubril, Muhammad 255

Kafrawi, Sa'id 256

Kamil, Mahmud 74

Kanafani, Ghassan 45, 75, 145, 281

Khalifah, Sahar 81

Kharrat, Idwar 127,177, 304

Khatib, Muhammad Kamil 317

Khedairi, Betool 297

Khuri, Ilyas 128, 178, 200, 224

Kuni, Ibrahim 303

Lashin, Mahmud Tahir 92

al-Lozi, Salim 37

Mahfuz, Najib 14, 22, 25, 38, 46, 49, 59, 76, 77, 78, 82, 93, 94, 101,116, 130, 131, 132, 153, 154, 170, 171, 172, 179, 180, 213, 225, 257, 283, 298, 306, 318, 319, 320

Mahmud, Mustafa 15

Mamduh, Aliyah 226

al-Mazini, Ibrahim 'Abd al-Qadir 34, 67

Minah, Hanna 181, 240

Mosteghanemi, Ahlem [Mustaghanimi, Ahlam] 284

Mu'alla, Abd al-Amir 50, 56

Munif, Abdelrahman 102, 118, 155, 183

Murr, Muhammad 156, 201

Musa, Sabri 57, 103, 215

Na'na', Hamidah 216

Nasir, Abd Allah Muhammad 321

Nasiri, Buthaynah 307

Nasr Allah, Ibrahim 184

Nasrallah, Emily 104, 173, 202

Nu'aymah, Mikha'il 4, 5, 31

al-Qa'id, Yusuf 95, 105, 241

Qasim, Abd al-Hakim 135, 217

al-Qusaybi, Ghazi Abd al-Rahman 227, 308

Rajab, Muna 309

Ramli, Muhsin 322

Rifaat, Alifa 68

Rizq, Abd al-Fattah 106, 242

Rushdi, Rashad 9

Saʻdani, Mahmud 119

al-Saʻdawi, Nawal 69, 84, 85, 107, 108, 120, 121, 136, 157, 186, 218, 299

Sabʻawi [Sabawi], Abd al-Karim 203

Salih, Tayeb [al-Tayyib] 18, 19, 58, 228

Salim, Ibtihal 311

al-Samman, Ghadah 219, 243, 260

al-Sharqawi, ʻAbd al-Rahman 8

Sharuni, Yusuf 70, 230

Shaykh, Hanan 96, 137, 204, 220, 231

Shukri, Muhammad 26, 233

al-Sibaʻi, Yusuf 27

Tahawi, Miral 261, 313

Tahir, Baha' 234, 312

Takarli, Fu'ad 300

Tamir, Zakariya 86

Tawfiq, Sahar 221

Taymur, Mahmud 2, 10, 187

Telmissany, May [Tilimsani, Mayy] 286

Tubya, Majid 122, 222

al-Tukhi, Abd Allah 314

Turjuman, Siham 205

Wadi, Taha ʻImran 244, 262

Waliyy al-Din, Ismaʻil 52

Wattar, al-Tahir 288

Yakhlif, Yahya 275

Yarid, Nazik Saba 245

Zangana, Haifa 159

al-Zayyat, Latifah 246, 289

Women Novelists[1]

Abu Zayd, Layla 123, 276

al-Amir, Daizy 188

Ashur, Radwa 315

Atrash, Layla 301

Attar, Samar 189, 248

Badr, Liyanah 124, 162, 190

Bakr, Salwa 163, 164, 208

Barakat, Huda 191, 291

Idlibi, Ulfat 212, 252

Khalifah, Sahar 81

Khedairi, Betool 297

Mamduh, Aliyah 226

Mosteghanemi, Ahlem [Mustaghanimi, Ahlam] 284

Na'na', Hamidah 216

al-Nasiri, Buthaynah 307

Nasrallah, Emily 104, 174, 202

Rajab, Muna 309

Ramadan, Sumayyah 310

Rifaat, Alifa 68

al-Sa'dawi, Nawal 69, 84, 85, 107, 108, 120, 121,136, 157, 186, 218, 299

al-Samman, Ghadah 219, 243, 260

al-Shaykh, Hanan 96, 137, 204, 220, 231

Tahawi, Miral 261, 313

Tawfiq, Sahar 221

Telmissany, May [Tilimsani, Mayy] 286

Turjuman, Siham 205

Yarid, Nazik Saba 245

Zangana, Haifa 159

al-Zayyat, Latifah 246, 289

---

1. For anthologies of short stories by Arab women writers see 175, 193, 206, 232, 273.

Translators Index

Abadir, Akef 25

Abd El-Nasser, Gamal 134, 255

Abdel Messih, Marie-Therese 105

Abdel Wahab, Farouk 15, 112, 236, 264, 312

Abou Hadid, Yussreya 313

Aboul Ela, Hosam 165

Abu Hassabo, Tagried 257

Akers, Deborah S. 273, 290

Allam, Suraya 209

Ali, Abd al-Mun'im 262

Allen, Roger 25, 38, 44, 80, 82, 123, 280, 286, 288

Alsebail, Abdulaziz 223

Asser, Martin 216

Attieh, Aman Mahmoud 232

Awad, Ramses Hanna 76

al-Ayouti, Amin 209

Ayyad, Hoda 103

Azrak, Michel 117

Badawi, M. M. 24, 41, 77

Bagader, Abu Bakr 140, 273, 290

Barakat, Maher 317

Basil, Rafik 160

Bell, Joseph 135

Bennett, Sophie 191, 246

Bishai, David 15

Booth, Marilyn 136,158, 221, 289, 291, 310, 311

al-Borollosy, Hala 166, 244

Bosio, Dina 321

Boullata, Issa 104, 223, 260, 302

Bowles, Paul 26

Bray, Robin 308, 316

Briggs, Jack 201

Brown, Clementina 240

Cachia, Pierre 269

Calderbank, Anthony 261, 296, 313, 320

Clark, Peter 156, 162, 212, 252

Cobham, Catherine 72, 121, 124, 137, 180, 220, 231, 300

Cohen-Mor, Dalya 151, 168, 175

Constable, Charlene 303

Cooke, Miriam 100, 146, 193

Cragg, Kenneth 6, 32

Daniel, Peter 88

Davies, Humphrey 318

Eban, Abba 1

Eber, Shirley 107, 108, 157

Ebied, R. W. 36

Elkhadem, Saad 113

Elmessiri, Abdel Wahab 129

Elmessiri, Nur 129

Emery, Ed 233

Enani, M. 255, 309

Enany, Rashid 94

Farghal, Muhammad 249

Fattouh, Essam 116

Fernea, Elizabeth 81

Ford, Peter 96

Frangieh, Bassam 141, 240

Frazier, W. McClung 21

El-Gabalawy, Saad 39, 51, 87, 89, 92, 111, 125, 152

Gafari, A. 308

Ghazoul, Ferial 303

Glubb, Faris 47

Gohar, Nadia 122

Gough, Jana 85

Granara, William 148, 288, 315

Grinsted, John Mohammed 126

Halwani, Nura 301

Hammond, Paul 159

Hancox, Stuart A. 245

Hannawi, Nay 294

Hantoosh, Yasmeen 322

Harlow, Barbara 75, 281

Harris, Russell 209

Hashem, Evine Mohamed 106

Hashem, Malak 77, 79, 130

Hassan Daoud 266

Hassan, Nirmeen 109

Hatim, Basil 298

Haydar, Adnan 70, 280

Haydar, Paula 178, 200, 224, 293

Heinrichsdorff, Ava Molnar 140, 273

Henry, Kristin Walker 93

Hetata, Sherif 63, 69, 84, 120, 186, 218

Hewison, R. Neil 271

Horan, Hume 10

Hutchins, William 67, 98, 132, 143, 153, 172, 211, 251

Iskandar, Marlyn 253

Islam, Mohamed 101

Ismail, Mohieddin 50

Jayyusi, May 145, 184, 194, 275, 305

Jayyusi, Salma Khadra 62

Johnson-Davies, Denys 2, 16, 18, 19, 20, 42, 66, 68, 70, 71, 86, 154, 164, 171, 192, 204, 213, 228, 235, 237, 256, 287, 307

Jones, Marsden 34

Kawar, Samira 190

Kennesson, James 118

Kenny, Lorne 95, 181

Kenny, Olive 78, 95, 132, 147, 181

Khalil-Khouri, Thoraya 174

Kilpatrick, Hilary 45

el Kommous, Maged 46

LeGassick, Trevor 14, 29, 40, 62, 74, 77, 81

Liardet, Frances 127, 150, 177

Liardet, Jean 179

Liechy, John 276

Lu'lu'a, A. W. 50, 56, 61

Manisty, Dinah 208

McGehee, Scott 141

McLoughlin, Leslie 32, 227

Mikhail, Mona N. 57

Morcos, Louis 7

Moussa-Mahmoud, Fatma 46

Mustafa, Farouk, see Abdel-Wahab, Farouk.

Naguib, Nawal 144

Naguib, Nayla 82, 99, 187, 197, 254

Naguib, Soad 238, 242

Nu'aymah, Mikha'il 4, 5

Nusairi, Osman 85

Parmenter, Barbara 123, 188

Perry, John 31

Peterson-Ishaq, Kristin 73

Porteous, Rebecca 202

Qanazi, Jurj 270

Qasimi, Ali 21

Reed, Jeremy 145, 147, 184

Riley, Karen 281

Roberts, Nancy 219, 229, 243

Rodenbeck, John 46, 77, 78

Romaine, Barbara 234

Rugh, Andrea 205

Rushdi, Rashad 9, 64

Saad El Din, Mursi 77, 253

El Sadda, Hoda 139, 163

Salameh, Fahd 182

Samaan, Angele Botros 172, 206

Salem, Nihad A. 27

al-Sanousi, Haifa 267

al-Sebail, Abdul-Aziz 273

Selaiha, Nehad 91

Shahbandar, Ghida 11

Shunnaq, Abd Allah 229, 249, 259

Shoukry, Mahmoud 28

Sobhi, Soad 116

St. Germain, May S. 303

St. Leger, Mona 53

Sreih, Baria Ahmar 284

Starkey, Paul 265

Stewart, Desmond 8, 12

Stewart, Philip 59

Stock, Raymond 306, 319

Tabet, Maia 128

Takla, George 241

Tanoukhi, Nirvana 292

Theroux, Peter 102, 155, 170, 183, 217, 225, 226, 247, 256

Tingley, Christopher 95, 162, 194, 275, 301, 321

Verlenden, John 304

Wahba, Magdi 33, 34, 101

al-Warraki, Nariman 93

Wassef, Wadida 43, 222

Wayment, Hilary 3

Watterson, Gavin 207

Williams, Malcolm 207, 298

Winder, R. Bayly 13

Woods, Macdara. 35

Young, M. J. L. 36, 117

El Zayyat, Mona 176, 199, 239

Titles Index

A Balcony over the Fakihani: Three Novellas ('A Land of Rock and Thyme', 'A Balcony over the Fakihani' and 'Canary and the Sea') 162

A Compass for the Sunflower 124

A Distress Call 238

A House Not her Own: Stories from Beirut 174

A Journey outside the Game 167

A Lake beyond the Wind 275

A Land of Rock and Thyme 162

A Land of Stone and Thyme: Palestinian Short Stories 129

A Last Glass of Tea and Other Stories 192

A Leader of Men 113

A Love Story 308

A Man of Letters 199

A New Year: Stories, Autobiography and Poems 31

A Passage to France: The Third Volume of the Autobiography of Taha Husain 33

A Period of Time 173

A Sad Tune on a Spanish Fiddle and Other Jordanian Short Stories 259

A Selection of Egyptian Short Stories 65

A Selection of Jordanian Short Stories 229

A Selection of Short Stories 22

A Sky So Close 297

A Touch of Fear 160

A Voice of their own: Short Stories by Egyptian Women 206

A Web of Stories: An Introduction to Short Fiction 263

A Woman of Five Seasons 301

Abu Foda 269

Adama 316

Adrift on the Nile 179

Afro–Asian Short Stories: An Anthology 23

Akhenaten, Dweller in Truth 257

al-Karnak 49

All That's Left to You: A Novella and Other Stories 145

Al-Mazini's Egypt [Includes *Midu and his Accomplices* and *Return to a Beginning*] 67

An Anthology of Modern Palestinian Literature 161

An Anthology of Moroccan Short Stories 207

An Arabian Mosaic: Short Stories by Arab Women Writers 175

Apartment Called Freedom 227

Arab Stories East and West 36

Arabian Nights and Days 213

Arabic Short Stories, 1945–1965 83

Arabic Short Stories 66

Arabic Writing Today: The Short Story 17

Assassination of Light: Modern Saudi Short Stories 140

Aunt Safiyya and the Monastery 234

Autumn Equinox 294

Autumn Quail 82, 283

Avant-Garde Egyptian Fiction: The Ulysses Trilogy 111

Bandarshah 228

Battlefront Stories from Iraq 61

Beirut '75 219

Beirut Blues 231

Beirut Nightmares 243

Bird of the East 13

Black Sky and Other Stories 119

Blood and Mud: Three Novelettes 269

Blood Feud 70

Blood into Ink: South Asian and Middle Eastern Women Write War 193

Blue Aubergine 313

Canadian Adventures of the Flying Egyptian 142

Canary and the Sea 162

Cat with Seven Lives 110

Charles, Diana, and Me and Other Stories 278

Children of Gebelawi 59

Children of the Alley 225

Children of the Waters 311

Cities of Salt 102

City of Love and Ashes 271

City of Saffron 127

City of Wrong: A Friday in Jerusalem 6

Daughter of Damascus 205

Days of Dust 29

Dear Mr Kawabata 265

Death in Beirut 32

Death of an Ex-Minister 107

Desire and Thirst: Egyptian Short Stories 262

Distant View of a Minaret and Other Stories 68

Dongola: A Novel of Nubia 247

Down to the Sea 150

Dubai Tales 156

Dunyazad 286

Egyptian Earth 8

Egyptian Short Stories 42

Egyptian Tales and Short Stories of the 1970s and 1980s 98

Egyptian Time 170

Endings 118

Eve without Adam 92

Evening Lake and Other Short Stories 139

Expanding Horizons: An Introduction to Non-Western Humanities 268

Final Night: Short Stories 307

Five Innovative Egyptian Short Stories 195

Flight against Time 104

Flights of Fantasy: Arabic Short Stories 79

For Bread Alone 26

Fountain and Tomb 116

Fragments of Memory: A Story of A Syrian Family 181

From the Travels of the Egyptian Odysseus 48

Fugitive Light 302

Gardens of the Night: A Trilogy 209

Gates of the City 178

Girls of Alexandria 177

Global Cultures: A Transnational Short Fiction Reader 198

Global Voices: Contemporary Literature from the Non-Western World 210

God Dies by the Nile 84

God's World 25

Good Morning! and Other Stories 100

Granada 315

Grandfather's Tale 252

Hommos Akhdar 52

Houses behind the Trees 237

I Am Free and Other Stories 40

I Sweep the Sun of Rooftops 204

Ibrahim the Writer 34

Improvisations on a Missing String 245

In Search of Walid Masoud 280

In the Eye of the Beholder. Tales of Egyptian Life 44

In the Tavern of Life and Other Stories 251

Incidents in Za'farani Alley 88

Iraqi Short Stories: An Anthology 114

Just Like a River 317

Khufu's Wisdom 319

Leaves of Narcissus 310

Libyan Stories: Twelve Short Stories from Libya 282

Lina: Portrait of a Damascene Girl 189

Literatures of Asia, Africa, and Latin America 272

Love in Exile 312

Love in the Kingdom of Oil 299

Maghreb: New Writing from North Africa 169

Mawardi Café 253

Maze of Justice 1

Memoirs of a Hen: A Present-Day Palestinian Fable 270

Memoirs of A Woman Doctor 121

Memory in Flesh 284

Men in the Sun and Other Palestinian Stories 45

Metaphysical Tales: Selected Short Stories 211

Midaq Alley, The Thief and the Dogs, Miramar 131

Midaq Alley 14

Miramar 46, 131

Mirrors 38

Modern Arab Stories 55

Modern Arabic Short Stories 16

Modern Egyptian Short Stories 7

Modern Egyptian Short Stories 39

Modern Egyptian Stories 134

Modern Iraqi Short Stories 21

Modern Jordanian Fiction: A Selection 182

Modern Literature of the Non-Western World: Where the Rivers Are Born 214

Modern Palestinian Short Stories in Translation 258

Modern Syrian Short Stories 117

Mothballs 226

News from the Meneisi Farm 105

Nine Short Stories 122

No One Sleeps in Alexandria 264

One Night in Cairo: An Egyptian Micronovel with Footnotes 295

Opening the Gates: A Century of Arab Feminist Writing 146

Palace of Desire: The Cairo Trilogy II 153

Palace Walk 132

Palestine's Children: Returning to Haifa and Other Stories 281

Palestine's Children: Short Stories 75

Paradise and the Accursed 106

Passage to Dusk 292

Passport to Arabia 185

Points of the Compass 221

Prairies of Fever 184

Rama and the Dragon 304

Ramadan Diary 109

Respected Sir 94

Respected Sir; Wedding Song; The Search 298

Return of the Spirit 143

Returning to Haifa 281

Rhadopis of Nubia 320

Rings of Burnished Brass: Short Stories 72

Rites of Assent 217

Sabriya: Damascus Bitter Sweet 212

Sara 41

Scattered Crumbs 322

Searching 157

Season of Migration to the North 19

Season of Migration to the North, and The Wedding of Zein 58

Seeds of Corruption 57, 215

Selected Egyptian Short Stories 64

Selected Stories and Essays 9

Selected Stories 151

Sensuous Lips and Other Stories 187

She Has No Place in Paradise 108

Sheikh Mursi Marries the Land: A Collection of Egyptian Short Stories 74

Short Fiction by Saudi Women Writers 232

Short Stories by Saudi Arabian Women Writers 273

Short Stories 309

Short Stories. Selections. The Piper Dies and Other Stories 168

Short Stories 166

The Short Story in the UAE 285

Six Days 141

Sixteen Sudanese Short Stories 60

Sleepless Nights 148

Stark Naked 242

Stars in the Sky of Palestine: Short Stories 47

Stories by Egyptian Women: My Grandmother's Cactus 158

Stories from the Rest of the World 138

Streetwise 233

Such a Beautiful Voice 163

Sugar Street 172

Sun on a Cloudy Day 240

Tales from Egyptian Life 2

The Beggar 93, 283

The Beggar; The Thief and the Dogs; Autumn Quail 283

The Beginning and the End 76

The Black Heaven and Other Stories 119

The Bleeding of the Stone 305

The Blind Lamp-Post and Other Stories 254

The Call of the Curlew 54

The Call of the Unknown 10

The Cheapest Nights and Other Stories 43

The Circling Song 136

The Cobbler and Other Stories 27

The Committee 303

The Day the Leader Was Killed 130

The Days of Drought 241

The Distant Horizon 244

The Dreams of Scheherazade 30

The Earthquake 288

The Echo of Kuwaiti Creativity: A Collection of Translated Short Stories 267

The Emigration to the North Country of Hathoot's Tribe 222

The Emigrés: A Novel 37

The Eye of the Mirror 190

The Eye with an Iron Lid 63

The Fall of the Imam 120

The Fantastic Strokes of Imagination 202

The Five Lovers 230

The Game of Forgetting 223

The Golden Chariot 208

The Gypsy 269

The Harafish 180

The Hill of Gypsies and Other Stories 256

The Homeland 216

The Hostage 194

The House of Mathilde 266

The House of Power 53

The House on 'Arnus Square 248

The Innocence of the Devil 218

The Journey of Ibn Fattouma 171

The Journey of Little Gandhi 200

The King of the Dead and Other Libyan Tales 35

The Kingdom of Strangers 224

The Language of Pain 144

The Last Chapter 276

The Literature of Modern Arabia: An Anthology 115

The Little Mountain 128

The Incident 103

The Long Days. 3 vols. Vols 1 and 2 50

The Long Days 56

The Long Way Back 300

The Man Who Lost his Shadow 12

The Memoirs of a Vagrant Soul, or the Pitted Face 4

The Modern Arabic Short Story: Shahrazad Returns 133

The Mountain of Green Tea 71

The Net 90

The Open Door 289

The Other Place 236

The Other Shore 255

The Owner of the House 246

The Phoenix 203

The Plague 125

The Postmaster 269

The Price of Sacrifice 11

The Right Man and Other Stories 197

The Rising from the Coffin 15

The River: A Tetralogy. Part One. 314

The Saint's Lamp and Other Stories 24

The Search 101, 298

The Searcher for the Truth 28

The Secret Life of Saeed, the Ill-fated Pessoptimist: A Palestinian Who Became a Citizen of Israel 62

The Seven Days of Man 135

The Sheltered Quarter: A Tale of Boyhood in Mecca 147

The Ship 80

The Sinners 73

The Slave's Dream and Other Stories 149

The Smell of It and Other Stories 20

The Square Moon: Supernatural Tales 260

The Stone of Laughter 191

The Story of Zahra 96

The Stream of Days: A Student at the Azhar 3

The Sufferers: Stories and Polemics 176

The Tears of a Nobody 99

The Tent 261

The Thief and the Dogs 77,131, 283

The Thread 186

The Tiller of Waters 291

The Time and the Place and Other Stories 154

The Tree and Other Stories 321

The Tree of Misery 239

The Trench 155

The Virgin of Dinshaway 89

The Waiting List: An Iraqi Woman's Tales of Alienation 188

The Wedding of Zein 58

The Wedding of Zein and Other Stories 18, 58

The Well of Life; and The Thread 186

The Wiles of Men and Other Stories 164

The Wings of Lead: A Modern Egyptian Novella 196

The Wink of Mona Lisa and Other Stories from the Gulf 201

The World of Literature 274

Thebes at War 318

They Die Strangers 290

This Side of Innocence 293

Three Contemporary Egyptian Novels 51

Three Egyptian Short Stories 152

Three Pioneering Egyptian Novels 97

Through the Vast Halls of Memory 159

Tigers on the Tenth Day and Other Stories 86

Till We Meet and Twelve Other Stories 5

Trial at Midnight 91

Two Avant-Garde Egyptian Novels; From Travels of the Egyptian Odysseus 250

Two Women in One 85

Ulysses's Hallucinations or the Like 87

Under the Naked Sky: Short Stories from the Arab World 287

Valley of Ashes 279

Variations on Night and Day 183

Voices from the Other World: Ancient Egyptian Tales 306

Voices 165

War in the Land of Egypt 95

Wedding Song 298

Wedding Song 78

When the Drums Beat: A Collection of Tunisian Short Stories 249

Who's Afraid of Agatha Christie? and Other Short Stories 277

Wild Thorns 81

Woman at Point Zero 69

Women of Sand and Myrrh 137

Writing through Literature 235

Year of the Elephant: A Moroccan Woman's Journey toward Independence and Other Stories 123

Zaat 296

Zainab 126

Zayni Barakat 112

Publishers Index

This index provides a general view of the role that different publishing institutions have played in promoting the translation of Arabic fiction since 1947. Of the nearly ninety publishers identified, only a small number can be credited with publishing five works or more. As the index and the bibliography itself indicate, small presses such as Heinemann, Interlink, Quartet Books, Saqi Books and Three Continents have been noted for their positive contribution to the translation of modern Arabic fiction, particularly between 1940s and 1980s.

Major commercial presses have not taken an active interest in publishing translated works of fiction prior to the 1980s. They have become more involved, though still in a limited way, since 1988. The same observation applies to the American University in Cairo Press (AUCP), which began to publish Arabic fiction in translation as early as 1984 but which increased its output after Najib Mahfuz was awarded the Nobel Prize for Literature. It has published thus far about forty works of fiction by Mahfuz and other Arab novelists.

Two other American institutions have made notable contributions: The Center for Middle Eastern Studies at the University of Texas and the University of Arkansas Press at Fayetteville. Arab institutions or publishing houses, public or private, in different Arab countries continue their tradition of sponsoring the translation and publication of Arabic works. Out of the 322 items listed in the bibliography, eighty or more works were published by Arab institutions, mainly in Egypt, illustrating the active part that Arab writers and institutions are increasingly playing in translating their literature into English and other Western languages. This is due in large measure to their feeling that Arabic literature has been ignored or marginalized in the West. However, significant as Arab contributions may seem, no assessment has yet been made of their success in selecting, translating and presenting modern Arabic literature to a wide audience beyond the Arab world.

Amman: Ministry of Culture 182

Austin, TX: Center for Middle Eastern Studies, The University of Texas 123, 145, 147, 181, 188, 223, 290, 292, 310

Austin, TX: University of Texas Press 1, 8, 158, 164, 205

Baghdad: Dar al Ma'mun for Translation and Publishing 50, 56, 61, 114

Baghdad: Ministry of Information 21

Bangalore, India: Indian Institute of World Affairs 5

Basingstoke, UK: Macmillan Press 133

Beirut: Khayats 10, 11, 13, 14

Beirut: Palestine Liberation Organization, Foreign Information Department 47

Berkeley, CA: University of California Press 66, 218, 234

Bloomington, IN: Indiana University Press 146

Boston, MA: Houghton Mifflin 12, 53, 57

Boulder, CO: Lynne Rienner 18, 19, 29, 43, 45, 192, 193, 251, 273, 281

Cairo, Giza: Egypt Foreign Press and Information Department, Ministry of Culture 65, 206

Cairo: American Research Center in Egypt 17

Cairo: Anglo–Egyptian Bookshop 7, 9, 64

Cairo: AUCP 76, 77, 78, 82, 83, 93, 98, 101, 132, 153, 172, 176, 179, 192, 199, 236, 237, 256, 257, 261, 264, 271, 284, 287, 289, 291, 296, 300, 303, 304, 306, 307, 310, 312, 313, 318, 319, 320

Cairo: Elias Modern Publishing House 79, 202

Cairo: GEBO 15, 30, 34, 40, 41, 74, 88, 91, 99, 103, 105, 106, 109, 110, 119, 122, 130, 134, 135, 139, 144, 160, 163, 166, 167, 187, 197, 215, 222, 230, 238, 241, 242, 244, 253, 254, 255, 262, 309, 314

Cairo: al-Maaref 3

Cairo: Palm Press 239

Cairo: Permanent Bureau of Afro–Asian Writers 23, 27

Cairo: Prism Publications 22

Cairo: Renaissance Bookshop 2

Cairo: Supreme Council for Islamic Affairs 28

Carthage/Tunis: Beit al-Hikma 148

Charlottetown, PEI, Canada: Gynergy Books 173

Charlottetown, PEI, Canada: Ragweed Press 104

Colorado Springs, CO: Three Continents Press 73, 189, 211, 232

Dubai, UAE: Motivate Publishing 201

Exeter, UK: Ithaca 151

Fayetteville, AR: University of Arkansas Press, 219, 221, 224, 245, 247, 260, 294, 322

Fredericton, NB, Canada: York Press 39, 51, 87, 89, 92, 97, 111, 113, 125, 142, 152, 195, 196

Irbid, Jordan: Dar al-Hilal 229, 249, 259

Jerusalem: The Palestinian Writers' Union 258

Kuwait: Centre for Research and Studies on Kuwait 267

Leeds: Leeds Oriental Society 36

Leiden: E. J. Brill 24, 31, 33, 54

London and New York: Cape Cod and Random House 102

London and New York: Penguin and Viking 112

London: Allison & Busby 37

London: Darf 126

London: Forest Books 156

London: G. Bles 6

London: Granta Books 266

London: Heinemann Educational Books 8, 12, 14, 16, 18, 19, 20, 32, 42, 43, 45, 46, 59, 68, 70, 71, 72, 75

London: Iraqi Cultural Centre 55

London: Kegan Paul 227, 228, 277, 278, 279, 282

London: Lime Tree 186

London: Longman, Green 3

London: Martin Brian and O'Keeffe 35

London: Methuen 107, 108, 120

London: Minerva 107, 108

London: Onyx Press 63

London: Oxford University Press 16

London: P. Owen 26

London: Quartet Books 32, 42, 43, 45, 46, 58, 66, 86, 94, 96, 118, 127, 129, 137, 149, 150, 158, 164, 175, 177, 209, 212, 223, 243, 246, 252, 265

London: Saqi 6, 8, 26, 81, 85, 95, 120, 121, 233, 286, 287, 288, 299, 308, 316

London: Serpent's Tail 185

London: The Harvill Press 1

London: The Women's Press 124

London: Zed Books 62, 69, 84, 90, 136, 157

Minneapolis, MN: Bibliotheca Islamica 25, 38, 44

Minneapolis, MN: University of Minnesota Press 128, 178, 200

New Delhi: Kali for Women 163

New York: Anchor Books 14, 46, 76, 96, 101, 130, 137, 179, 220, 231, 257, 283, 298

New York: Columbia University Press 161

New York: Doubleday 132, 153, 154, 170, 171, 172, 180, 213, 225

New York: Interlink Books 162, 184, 194, 275, 293, 301, 305, 317, 321

New York: Marion Boyars Publishers 165

New York: Palgrave Macmillan 133

New York: Pantheon Books 155, 183, 297

New York: Philosophical Library 4

New York: Quality Paperback Book Club 131

New York: Seabury Press 6

New York: Vintage Press 62, 102, 155, 183, 231

Oxford: Oneworld 6

Paris: Hourglass 159

Philadelphia, PA: Temple University Press 217

Potomac, MD: Sheba Press 168, 174

Pueblo, CO: Passeggiata Press 59, 240, 248, 269

Reading, UK: Garnet 190, 191, 208, 216, 226

Rockport, MA: Oneworld 6

San Francisco: City Lights Books 26

St. Leonards, Australia: Allen & Unwin 204

Syracuse, NY: Syracuse University Press 208, 302, 315

Tangier: King Fahd's School of Translation, Abdelmalek Essaadi University 207

Toronto, Ont.: York Press 250, 270, 295

United Arab Emirates: Ministry of Information and Culture 285

Upper Ferntree Gully, Victoria, Australia: Papyrus Publishing House 203

Washington, DC: Embassy of the Democratic Republic of the Sudan, Office of the Cultural Counselor 60

Washington, DC: Three Continents Press 12, 14, 16, 18, 19, 29, 32, 42, 45, 46, 59, 67, 75, 80, 100, 116, 117, 140, 141, 143, 192 (See also Colorado Springs)

Wilmette, IL: Medina Press International 29

Winchester, MA: Faber and Faber 129

York, UK: Talus Editions, University of York 169

Countries Index

Arab World 16, 17, 23, 36, 55, 66, 79, 83, 115, 133, 138, 146, 185, 198, 174, 193, 210, 214, 272, 287

Algeria 284, 288

Egypt 1, 2, 3, 6, 7, 8, 9, 10, 12, 13, 14, 15, 20, 22, 24, 25, 27, 28, 30, 33, 34, 38, 39, 40, 41, 42, 43, 44, 46, 48, 49, 51, 53, 54, 57, 59, 63, 64, 65, 67, 68, 69, 70, 71, 72, 73, 74, 76, 77, 78, 82, 84, 85, 87, 88, 89, 90, 91, 93, 94, 95, 98, 99, 100, 101, 103, 105, 106, 107, 108, 109, 110, 111, 112, 113, 116, 119, 120, 122, 125, 126, 127, 130, 131, 132, 134, 135, 136, 137, 139, 142, 143, 149, 150, 151, 152, 153, 154, 157, 160, 163, 164, 165, 166, 167, 168, 170, 171, 172, 173, 176, 177, 179, 180, 184, 186, 187, 192, 195, 196, 197, 199, 206, 208, 211, 215, 217, 218, 221, 222, 225, 230, 234, 236, 237, 238, 239, 241, 242, 244, 246, 247, 250, 251, 253, 254, 255, 256, 261, 262, 264, 269, 271, 283, 286, 289, 295, 296, 298, 303, 304, 306, 309, 310, 311, 312, 313, 314, 315, 318, 319, 320

Iraq 21, 50, 56, 61, 114, 159, 188, 226, 297, 300, 307, 322

Jordan 182, 229, 259

Kuwait 267

Lebanon 4, 5, 29, 31, 32, 37, 96, 104, 128, 137, 141, 174, 178, 200, 202, 204, 220, 224, 231, 245, 265, 266, 291, 292, 293, 294

Libya 35, 209, 277, 278, 279, 282, 304

Morocco 26, 123, 169, 207, 223, 233, 276, 302

Palestine 45, 47, 62, 75, 80, 81, 124, 129, 145, 161, 162, 184, 190, 191, 203, 216, 228, 270, 275, 280, 281, 300

Saudi Arabia 11, 102, 118, 140, 147, 155, 183, 227, 232, 273, 308, 316, 321

Sudan 18, 19, 58, 60, 228

Syria 86, 117, 181, 189, 205, 212, 219, 240, 248, 252, 260, 317

Tunisia 148, 249

United Arab Emirates 156, 201, 285

Yemen 194, 290

CHAPTER FOUR

Arabic Poetry: An Overview of Selected Anthologies

It is generally recognized that poetry as the primary genre in Arabic literature has been only marginally represented in English translations; in studies of Islam or the Arab world it has been largely ignored until recently. Of more than two thousand modern poems translated into English during the twentieth century, only about fifty were published before 1950. In addition, the translation, in nearly all cases, was done by native speakers of Arabic. A number of factors, including negative attitudes, account for this marginal representation of poetry; I have alluded to these in the chapter on Najib Mahfuz. However, it is important to note that earlier British and American Orientalists/Arabists were more concerned with non-literary aspects of the Arab world and thus failed to engage actively in the translation of modern poetry or other Arabic literary genres. The only notable exception was Arthur Arberry, whose contributions to the translation of poetry, both classical and modern, included his pioneering 1950 anthology.

As Arberry pointed out in his preface to the anthology, he and students from several Arab countries cooperated to produce a collection representative of Arabic poetry written between 1920 and the 1940s. Arberry's versified translations may strike readers of poetry as artificial and ineffective in achieving the poetic quality of the originals; but by choosing versification he raised an important issue about the methodology of translating poetry. He obviously felt that his translations should reflect the poetic styles and techniques of the original poems. Its stylistic flaws aside, Arberry's anthology was a positive contribution to the translation of modern Arabic poetry because it was a collaborative effort between Arabic- and English-speaking translators and because of its broad scope in terms of the poets and the countries represented (forty-five poets, eleven countries and the two schools of Arab poets active in the United States and South America).

Following the publication of the anthology and until the early 1970s, slow but steady strides were made in the translation of Arabic poetry, particularly in the US. However, the translations appeared mostly in journals and little magazines. Moreover, in spite of these strides and the proliferation of Arabic studies in American and British institutions, no other anthology comparable to Arberry's was published. It was only during the 1970s and 1980s that we begin to witness the publication of more significant and diversified anthologies of Arabic poetry in English translation. They were edited or undertaken not only in English-speaking countries (mainly the UK and USA) but also in several Arab countries, such as Egypt, Iraq and Lebanon. This latter fact underlines the prominent role that Arab translators have played in ensuring that Arabic poetry reaches a wider audience and receives the recognition it deserves as part of world literature. Whether working alone or in cooperation with English-speaking translators, Arab translators (poets, scholars and others) have contributed, though not always successfully, to most of the translations that are currently available (see, for example, Altoma 13–16).

Apart from the innumerable translated poems published in periodicals and in studies dealing with Arabic literature, there are now numerous anthologies, which represent the poetry of the postwar period. These can be classified into three categories: A) General/Pan-Arab anthologies; B) Region- or country-oriented anthologies; and C) Anthologies of poets.

For the purpose of this survey, we will be looking at the scope and method of translation of representative anthologies of the first group only.

Khouri and Algar's bilingual anthology (1974) offers a fine and reliable translation of eighty poems by thirty-five poets. The poetry selected represents mostly the post-1950 free verse and prose poem movements, but it also includes examples from the works of leading pre-1950 poets who were known for their innovations or departure from the classical tradition. Issa Boullata's (1976) focuses on the former movement and captures, with remarkable skill, the spirit of the period (1950–1975) as manifested in the works of twenty-two poets. Both anthologies cover countries where the new currents first emerged: Egypt, Iraq, Lebanon, Palestine, Syria and the Sudan. Khouri's collection includes, in addition, a noted romantic poet from Tunisia, al-Shabbi (1909–34). However, both anthologies, useful and reliable as they are, lack the poetic quality that only creative translators in the target language can ensure.

Jayyusi's Project for Translation from Arabic (PROTA) has sought to address this problem by enlisting the contribution of English-speaking poets in several of the anthologies she has edited since the early 1980s. Her *Modern*

Arabic Poetry (1987), in particular, stands out as a landmark in the history of Arabic poetry in English translation, for several reasons.

First, as a leading poet and authority on the subject, Jayyusi has carefully chosen a large number of poems that represent the various phases of modern Arabic poetry, ranging from the neoclassical to the more recent and radical transformation that Arabic poetry has undergone. The anthology includes examples (sometimes excerpts or fragments) from the works of more than ninety poets, arranged into two broadly defined sections: poets before and after the 1950s. Second, as a testament to the pan-Arab unity of culture and spirit, Jayyusi's collection provides a broader geographical representation by including poets from different parts of the Arab world (from the Gulf to the Atlantic), though more poets are still drawn, for understandable reasons, from Egypt and the Fertile Crescent region (Iraq, Jordan, Lebanon, Syria and Palestine). Third, the anthology has succeeded to a large measure in providing a truly poetic translation of the original text, thanks to the participation of a number of American, British, Canadian and Irish poets: Alan Brownjohn, Patricia Alanah Byrne (Rosenfield), Diana Der Hovanessian, Charles Doria, Alistair Eliot, Thomas Ezzy, Samuel Hazo, John Heath-Stubbs, W. S. Merwin, Christopher Middleton, Naomi Shihab Nye, Desmond O'Grady, Peter Porter, Anthony Thwaite and Richard Wilbur. This was achieved in cooperation with a group of first translators competent in both Arabic and English.

There is an obvious literary benefit in enlisting the help of creative translators in the target language, not only because of their rootedness in the poetics of their literary tradition and their first-hand familiarity with the literary taste of their time, but also because they are more qualified to serve as effective intermediaries between their own culture and that of the source language. Such an approach does have, as some critics maintain, its own potential risk in that it may lead to inaccurate rewriting of the original poems. However, inaccuracies in Jayyusi's anthology are rare, though in some cases, especially with traditional poetry, the original poems have been deliberately truncated or abridged. For example, the translated version of 'Lullaby for the Hungry', by the greatest modern neoclassical poet, Muhammad Mahdi al-Jawahiri (1900–1997), is based on twenty lines selected from a much longer (one hundred-line) poem. But, as Jayyusi herself stated, such neoclassical poetry presents the translator with a most onerous task as it is built on well-entrenched phrases and a rich legacy of rhetorical usages and other devices, which are not translatable without the aid of unwieldy footnotes. Instead of excluding the translation of traditional poetry, which still plays a central role in the Arab world, Jayyusi has wisely attempted to represent it in her anthology in abridged versions.

Other general anthologies, which deserve to be noted, include al-Udhari's *Modern Poetry of the Arab World* (1986), which presents, according to a chronological and theme-oriented scheme, works of leading poets from the Fertile Crescent region: Iraq, Jordan/Palestine, Lebanon and Syria. The selections are grouped under four headings: the Taf'ila (free verse) movement (Iraqi School), 1947–57; the Majallah Shi'r Movement (Syrian School), 1957–67; the June (i.e., June War of 1967) Experience, 1967–82; and the Beirut Experience (i.e., Israel's occupation of Beirut), 1982 onwards. As the headings suggest, Udhari's anthology brings together some of the finest modernist poets who are known for their poetic innovations and radical stand against political and social conditions in the Arab world. Among the poets represented are Adonis, al-Bayati, Darwish, Hawi, Jabra, al-Khal, al-Maghut, Qabbani, al-Sayyab and Sa'di Yusuf. However, Udhari's schemes of classification or periodization and of selection can be questioned on several grounds, such as limited regional representation (despite the title) and the fact that not all of his selections belong to the periods under which they are included.

John Asfour's *When the Words Burn: An Anthology of Modern Arabic Poetry 1945-1987* is a slightly revised version of his dissertation, 'An Anthology of Modern Arabic Poetry 1945–1984 with a Critical Introduction'. It is noted for its well-researched, incisive and informative coverage of modern/modernist poets during the period. This is reflected not only in the introduction (pp.14-73), which deals with pre-1945 and various innovative movements and in the bibliographical sources (227–237) but also in Asfour's sensitive choice of poets and poems. The latter are organized under three main sections: The Free Verse Movement (A. A Generation of Departures. B. Explorations in Modern Forms and Idioms); Tammuz Rediscovered (A. Five Major Tammuzi Poets. B. In the Tammuzi Tradition); Resistance Poetry.

As a talented poet in English and a student of Arabic poetry, Asfour has carefully chosen for his anthology thirty-five poets, some of whom are not included in other collections, such as Salim Haqqi, Khalid al-Khazraji, Ghadah al-Samman, Shadhil Taqah and Michel Trad. Trad writes in the Lebanese dialect, but is included primarily because of his outstanding contribution to Lebanese folk poetry. A concise and useful biographical note introduces each poet. The anthology is not as representative in geographical terms as Jayyus's work, focusing as it does, for understandable academic reasons, on poets from the Arab East, namely Bahrain, Egypt, Iraq, Lebanon, Palestine, Sudan and Syria, without reference to important developments in North African countries of Algeria, Libya, Morocco and Tunisia. Nonetheless, the anthology is a highly illuminating and reliable source for both specialists and general readers interested in modern Arabic poetry.

Anne Fairbairn's bilingual anthology (1989) represents an ambitious undertaking by two poets: Fairbairn herself, an Australian, and Ghazi al-Gosaibi (or al-Qusaybi), a Saudi poet of distinction, who is also noted for his contributions to other projects of translation as well as for his critical studies of Arabic poetry. Intended primarily as an introduction for Australian readers, the anthology aims to provide a panorama of twentieth-century Arabic poetry. Three criteria guided Fairbairn and al-Gosaibi's choice: the poems should come from every Arab country; they should represent different schools, with the exception of prose poetry; and the poems should have universal themes 'such as poverty, death, love, parenthood' (Introduction, n. p.). In spite of the obstacles inherent in such an undertaking, the editors/translators have succeeded in offering a large number of selections, often of just a few lines, from the works of more than ninety poets. Most of the poets chosen belong to the post-1950 generations. Fairbairn attempted different versions of translation on the basis of al-Gosaibi's liberal translations. Being a poet herself, she was guided by the principle that her translations should re-create the original texts in English without distorting their essence. The result is a sampling of poems perceptively selected from Arabic and artistically rendered in English. The leading Australian poet A. D. Hope (1907–2000) greeted it within the Australian context as 'a miraculous achievement' and 'a literary event' that would 'help to break down those barriers which so sadly divide us today' (Foreword, n. p.).

In 1998 Margaret Obank along with Samuel Shimon published in London the first issue of *Banipal*, a magazine dedicated to the translation and promotion of modern Arab literature. Since then, *Banipal* has published more than a hundred poems and other works in translation. Based on their experience with the growing interest in modern Arabic poetry, they decided to collect in one volume sixty poets from the hundred or more whose work had been translated and published between 1998 and 2000.

Entitled *A Crack in the Wall: New Arab Poetry* (2001), the collection stands out as a departure from all other anthologies discussed earlier for a number of reasons. First, it is not the outcome of a pre-defined project aimed at selecting poetry for translation with a specific objective in mind. It is based mainly on the choices of some eighteen translators who published their translations in *Banipal* between 1998 and 2000. As a result, what is called 'New Arab Poetry' is unevenly represented in the anthology. Most of the sixty poets chosen live in exile, about ten write in English or French, most were born after the Second World War, whereas others belong to earlier generations, and many other poets are left out for a variety of reasons. The sixty poets were chosen primarily because their works were published between 1980 and 2000. Poetry by writers such as Adonis and al-Sayyab, which appeared in *Banipal*, was excluded because it was originally written before the 1980s. However, nearly all Arab countries are represented by one or more poets.

Apart from such reservations, one cannot but be impressed with the overall quality of the poets selected for this anthology. They are noted for their daring and innovative stylistic features, for the breadth and diversity of themes they reflect, ranging from personal anguish, alienation, love and exile to social or political events or changes (national or international), which they have experienced in recent decades, for their universal outlook and for the remarkable positive spirit that prevails, here and there, against a world of cruelty, violence and injustice. The fact that many of the poets in this collection have lived in and directly interacted with Western societies (Europe, Australia and the United States) may have contributed in various ways to their innovative spirit. Two other important features should be pointed out. First, unlike in other anthologies, most of the poets here are represented for the first time. Only eight out of the sixty, for example, are included in Jayyusi's fairly comprehensive and representative work. Second, the poems were mostly translated by well-known translators (scholars or poets) such Jareer Abu-Haydar, Sargon Boulus, Adnan Haydar, Paul Haydar, James Kirkup, Khaled Mattawa (who translated about fifteen poets) and Anton Shammas.

All the anthologies cited above include the works of several women poets; but Kamal Boullata's anthology (1978) is dedicated exclusively to Arab women's contributions to the poetic revolution that has taken place during the last fifty years. Among the thirteen poets represented are Nazik al-Mala'ikah (Iraq), Salma Khadra Jayyusi and Fadwa Tuqan (Palestine) and Fawziyya Abu Khalid (Saudi Arabia). Although not comprehensive in its coverage of women poets, Boullata's work still serves as an important guide to the creative spirit of Arab women as they address personal, national and universal problems of their time. It includes about a hundred poems or extracts of poems, mostly translated from Arabic, but in some cases translated from French or originally written in English. The English translations from Arabic, primarily by Boullata, are notable for both artistic sensitivity and reliability. The fact that they have appeared in major world anthologies of women's poetry may serve as a measure of their success.

In contrast to Boullata's pioneering collection, Handal's recent anthology (2001) is a more comprehensive work that seeks to ensure a greater visibility not only for Arab women poets but also for other poets who are of Arab origin. International in its scope, the anthology presents the works of eighty-three poets, most of whom write in Arabic and are chosen from all Arab countries with the exception of Oman and the Sudan. The second largest group is that of the Arab–American poets, followed by others who write in French or Swedish. By bringing together in one volume poets from different

Arab and non-Arab regions, literary traditions and religious backgrounds, Handal has succeeded to a large extent in demonstrating some of the writers' shared experiences and concerns. The anthology begins with a detailed introduction (more than sixty pages), which sheds light on salient stylistic and thematic aspects of Arab women's poetry as it evolved during the twentieth century. It concludes with biographical notes about the poets and the numerous translators (about forty), including American, Australian and British poets, who contributed to the anthology. The greater visibility of Arab women poets is also reflected in the publication of an increasing number of their individual works (see, for example, titles listed below under Kashghari, al-Sabah, Sa'd, Saudi and Tuqan).

As this survey shows, an extensive corpus of contemporary Arabic poetry has become accessible in English translation in a variety of sources, including numerous anthologies. Extensive as it is, however, it offers only a partial representation of Arabic poetry today. There are many poets who have been inadequately represented or left out completely. Al-Babatin's (1995) dictionary of living poets alone lists more than 1,600 poets, selected from a much larger number of poets participating in a special survey. This is not to imply that all poets listed merit serious consideration for the purpose of translation. It suggests only that there is still a major gap in the corpus of translated poetry. This gap is particularly evident in relation to the contemporary poetry of North African countries – Algeria, Libya, Morocco and Tunisia. It is also evident in the absence of individual collections representing other major modern poets such as Amal Dunqul and Ahmad Abd al-Mu'ti Hijazi (Egypt), Salma Khadra Jayyusi and Tawfiq Sayigh (Palestine), Nazik al-Mala'ikah and Badr Shakir al-Sayyab, (Iraq) Abd al-Aziz al-Maqalih (Yemen) and Yusuf al-Khal (Lebanon).

What is more noteworthy, perhaps, is the fact that while non-Arabic speaking-translators have become more involved in the translation of modern Arabic poetry, native Arabic speakers continue to serve as the primary anthologists. There are a few notable exceptions, such as the American poet Samuel Hazo, who translated Adonis; Denys Johnson-Davies, known for his translation of numerous Arabic works including Mahmud Darwish's poetry; and Desmond O'Grady, as the bibliography below indicates. A fairly large number of the collections have been published in Arab countries, particularly Egypt, a fact that may limit their circulation or use in English-speaking countries.

Further Reading

Altoma, Salih J., *Modern Arabic Poetry in English Translation: A Bibliography* Tangier: King Fahd School of Translation, Abdelmalek Essaadi University, 1993 [For more information on other anthologies not discussed above or listed below, see 13–16, 146–49].

Bibliography

Pan-Arab Anthologies

Arberry, Arthur J., *Modern Arabic Poetry: An Anthology with English Verse Translations* London: Taylor's Foreign Press, 1950; Cambridge: Cambridge University Press, 1967.

Asfour, John Mikhail, *When the Words Burn: An Anthology of Modern Arabic Poetry, 1947–1987* Dunvegan, Ont.: Cormorant Books, 1988; revised edition, 1992.

Boullata, Issa J., *Modern Arab Poets: 1950–1970* Washington, DC: Three Continents Press, 1976.

Boullata, Kamal, *Women of the Fertile Crescent: Modern Poetry by Arab Women* Washington, DC: Three Continents Press, 1978; Boulder, CO: Lynne Rienner, 1981, 1994.

Fairbairn, Anne, and Ghazi al-Gosaibi, *Feathers and the Horizon: A Selection of Modern Arabic Poetry from Across the Arab World* Canberra: Leros Press, 1989.

Handal, Nathalie, ed., *The Poetry of Arab Women: A Contemporary Anthology* New York; Northampton, MA: Interlink Books, 2001.

Jayyusi, Salma Khadra, ed., *Modern Arabic Poetry: An Anthology* New York: Columbia University Press, 1987.

Megally, Shafik, trans., *An Anthology of Modern Arabic Poetry* Zug: International Documentation Co., 1974.

Obank, Margaret and Samuel Shimon, ed., *A Crack in the Wall: New Arab Poetry* London: Saqi, 2001.

O'Grady, Desmond, *Ten Modern Arab Poets: Selected Versions* Dublin: The Dedalus Press, 1992 [Includes all the modern poets covered in his anthology *Trawling Tradition: Translations 1954–1994* Salzburg: University of Salzburg, 1994 (see below under International Anthologies), with the exception of Fadwa Tuqan. In addition, O'Grady chose to include in this anthology a classical poet, Abu Nuwas (747–810?)].

Samples of Modern Arabic Poetry in English Translation, trans. Lana Younis; revised with an introduction by Muhammad Enani. Cairo: GEBO, 1999 [Inside title, *Exercises in Translation: Poem [Poetry] and Prose*, is more accurate in view of the fact that the samples include not only poems by Adonis, Badr Shakir al-Sayyab, Jabra I. Jabra, Muhammad al-Maghut and Ahmad Abd al-Mu'ti Hijazi but also two plays by Alfred Faraj and a few selections from an earlier period].

al-Udhari, Abdullah, trans., *Modern Poetry of the Arab World* Harmondsworth, UK: Penguin Books, 1986.

Selected Regional Anthologies

Ahmed, Osman Hassan, and Constance E. G. Berkley, eds, *Anthology of Modern Sudanese Poetry* Washington, DC: Office of the Cultural Counselor, Embassy of the Democratic Republic of the Sudan, 1983.

Aruri, Naseer, and Edmund Ghareeb, eds, *Enemy of the Sun, Poetry of Palestinian Resistance* Washington, DC: Drum and Spear Press, 1970

Elmessiri, A. M., trans., *The Palestinian Wedding: A Bilingual Anthology of Contemporary Palestinian Resistance Poetry* Washington, DC: Three Continents Press, 1982.

—— *A Lover from Palestine and Other Poems: An Anthology of Palestinian Poetry* Washington, DC: Free Palestine Press, 1970.

Enani, M. M., trans., *An Anthology of the New Arabic Poetry in Egypt* Cairo: General Egyptian Book Organization, 1986.

—— *Angry Voices: An Anthology of the Off-Beat New Egyptian Poets* Fayetteville, AR: University of Arkansas Press, 2003.

Ghanem, Shihab, trans., *Modern Poetry from the Land of Sheba* United Arab Emirates: N.P. [Sh. M. A. Ghanem], 1999 [Dubai, UAE: Deira Printing Press, author's responsibility].

—— *Pearls and Shells* Dubai, UAE: Deira Printing Press, 1996 [author's responsibility, poems from the UAE].

—— *20th Century Poetry from Palestine* Sharjah, UAE: Department of Culture, 2001.

Ghazzawi, Izzat, ed., *Modern Palestinian Poetry in Translation: 35 Poets* Jerusalem: The Palestinian Writers' Union, 1997.

Jayyusi, Salma Khadra, ed., *Anthology of Modern Palestinian Literature* New York: Columbia University Press, 1992. See pp. 81–331 for translations of Arabic poems by fifty-seven Palestinian poets.

—— ed., *Literature of Modern Arabia: An Anthology* London and New York: Kegan Paul International, 1988. See pp. 41–252 for poetry in translation from Bahrain, Kuwait, Oman, Qatar, Saudi Arabia, United Arab Emirates and Yemen.

Kaye, Jacqueline, ed., *Maghreb: New Writing from North Africa* York, UK: Talus Editions and University of York, 1992 [Includes poems by four Moroccan poets: Ahmed Belbdaoui, Muhammad Bennis, Ahmad al-Majjati and Abd Allah Raji'].

Lu'lu'a, Abdul Wahid, trans., *Modern Iraqi Poetry* Baghdad: Dar al-Ma'mun, 1989.

Megalli, Shafik, trans., *Arab Poetry of Resistance: An Anthology* Cairo: al-Ahram Press, 1970.

Palestinian Roses: Incarnadine: Selection of Poetry Published by Ad-Dustour Newspaper, trans. Daud Ghuneim. Amman: Majdalawi, 1987.

Poetic Experimentation in Egypt since the Seventies. Alif (Cairo: AUCP) 11 (1991) [A special issue, which presents a bilingual anthology of poems selected from the works of about twenty contemporary Egyptian poets].

Poetic Lebanon. Photographs by Paddy Tchrakian and Richard Manoukian. Poetry selected and translated by Yusuf al-Khal. Beirut: Khayats, 1965 [Not an anthology, but a small memento of photographs and one-line verses selected from the works of numerous poets, mostly Lebanese, and translated by al-Khal, 1917–1987].

Rebellious Voices: Selection of Poetry by Arab Women Writers in Jordan, ed. and trans. Abd Allah Shahham. Amman: A. A. Shahham, 1988 [Includes selected poems by Amina al-Adwan and Shahla al-Kayyali].

al-Sanousi, Haifa, trans., *The Echo of Kuwaiti Creativity: A Collection of Translated Kuwaiti Poetry* [Revised by Mohammad Sami Anwar]. Kuwait: Center for Research and Studies on Kuwait, 1999.

Selection of Contemporary Iraqi Poetry, trans. George Masri. London: Iraqi Cultural Centre, 1977 [Poems by Buland al-Haydari, Shafiq al-Kamali and Hamid Sa'id].

Shahham, Abd Allah, trans., *Symphonies of the Heart: Selections from Modern Arabic Poetry in Jordan* Amman: Department of Culture and Arts, 1987.

al-Wasiti, Salman, ed., *Ten Iraqi Soldier–Poets* Baghdad: Dar al-Ma'mun, 1988 [Covers the Iran–Iraq War].

With Stones They Pave the Path to Liberty; and Other Poems of the Intifadah. Selected and trans. Thoraya Mahdi Allam. [S. I.] Palestine Liberation Organization, Department of Culture, 1990?

Selected Anthologies of Poets

Abd al-Wahid, Abd al-Razzaq, *Poems*. Selected by Ali Ja'far Allaq and trans. Mohammed Darweesh. Baghdad: Dar al-Ma'mun, 1989.

Abu Sinna, Muhammad Ibrahim, *Poems*, trans. Soad Mahmoud Naguib and Mahir Shafiq Farid. Cairo: GEBO, 1993.

Adonis (Ali Ahmad Sa'id), *The Blood of Adonis: Transpositions of Selected Poems of Adonis* (Ali Ahmad Said), trans. Samuel Hazo. Pittsburgh, PA: University of Pittsburgh Press, 1971.

―――― *If Only the Sea Could Sleep*, trans. Mirene Ghossin, Kamal Boullata and Susan L. Einbinder. Copenhagen; Los Angeles, CA: St Paul, MN: Green Integer, 2003.

―――― *The Pages of Day and Night*, trans. Samuel Hazo. Marlboro, VT: Marlboro Press, 1994; Evanston, IL: Marlboro Press; Northwestern University Press, 2000.

―――― *Transformations of the Lover*, trans. Samuel Hazo. Athens, OH: Ohio University Press, 1983.

Afif, Qaysar, *The Trilogy of Exile*, trans. Mansour Ajami, ed. Barbara De Graff Ajami. [California?: s. n.]: 2000.

―――― *And the Word Became Poem*, trans. Mansour Ajami, ed. Barbara De Graff Ajami. Princeton, NJ: The Grindstone Press, 1994.

Ali, Taha Muhammad, *Never Mind: Twenty Poems and A Story*, trans. Peter Cole et al. Jerusalem: Ibis Editions, 2000.

al-Allaq, Ali Ja'far, *Poems*, trans. Mohammed Darweesh. Baghdad: Dar al-Ma'mun, 1988.

Arar, see al-Tall, Mustafa Wahbi.

Awaji, Ibrahim, *The Tents of the Tribe*, trans. Maryam Ishaq al-Khalifa Sharief. London: Echoes, 1996.

al-Azzawi, Fadil, *In Every Well a Joseph Is Weeping*, trans. Khaled Mattawa. *Quarterly Review of Literature. Poetry Book Series* 36 (1997).

―――― *Miracle Maker: Selected Poems*, trans. Khaled Mattawa. Rochester, NY: BOA Editions, 2003.

Baini, Charbel, *Quartets Rubaiyat*, trans. Emile Chidiac. Merrylands, Australia: Charbel Baini, 1993.

al-Bayati, Abd al-Wahhab, *Love, Death, and Exile*, trans. Bassam K. Frangieh. Washington, DC: Georgetown University Press, 1990.

Algosaibi, see al-Qusaybi.

Darwish, Mahmud, *The Adam of Two Edens*, eds Munir Akash and Daniel Moore. Bethesda, MD: Jusoor; Syracuse, NY: Syracuse University Press, 2001.

—— *From Beirut*, trans. Stephen Kessler. Albion, CA: Pygmy Forest Press, 1992 [A translation based, according to Kessler, on 'a Spanish version by Ikram Antaki [published] in the Mexico City magazine *Plural* in 1983'].

—— *The Music of Human Flesh*, trans. Denys Johnson-Davies. London: Heinemann Educational Books; Washington, DC: Three Continents Press, 1980.

—— *Psalms*, trans. Ben Bennani. Colorado Springs, CO: Three Continents Press, 1994.

—— *Sands and Other Poems*, trans. Rana Kabbani. London: Kegan Paul International, 1986, 2001.

—— *Selected Poems*, trans. Ian Wedde and Fawwaz Tuqan. Cheshire, UK: Carcanet Press, 1973.

—— *Splinters of Bone*, trans. Ben Bennani. Greenfield Center, N.Y: Greenfield Review Press, 1974.

—— .*Unfortunately, it Was Paradise: Selected Poems*, trans. Munir 'Akash and Carolyn Forché. Berkeley, CA: University of California Press, 2003.

al-Faytouri, see Fituri.

Fituri, Muhammad, *Shrouded by the Branches of Night*, trans. Muhammad Enani. Cairo: GEBO, 1997.

Ghanem, Shihab, *Shades of Love*, trans. by the author. Dubai, UAE: Deira Printing Press, 1995 [Author's responsibility].

Guwaidah, Farooq, see Juwaydah, Faruq.

Hafidh, Yaseen Taha, see Hafiz, Yasin Taha.

Hafiz, Hisham Ali, *The Desert Is my Oasis* London: Kegan Paul, 1994.

—— *Words with Rhythm: Second Beat*, trans. Farouk Luqman. London: Kegan Paul, 1995.

Hafiz, Yasin Taha, *War: A Long Poem*, trans. Shihab Ahmad al-Nasir. Baghdad: Dar al-Ma'mun, 1988.

—— *Poems*, trans. Mohammed Darweesh. Baghdad: Dar al-Ma'mun, 1989.

Hawi, Khalil and Nadeem Naimy, *From the Vineyards of Lebanon*, trans. Fuad Said Haddad. Beirut: The American University of Beirut, 1991.

Hawi, Khalil, *Naked in Exile: Khalil Hawi's Threshing Floors of Hunger*, trans. Adnan Haydar and Michael Beard. Washington, DC: Three Continents Press, 1984.

al-Haydari, Buland, *Songs of the Tired Guard*, trans. Abdullah al-Udhari. London: TR Press, 1977.

—— *Dialogue in Three Dimensions*, trans. Husain Haddawy. London: Pan Middle East Graphics and Publishing, 1982.

al-'Isa, Sulayman, *The Butterfly and Other Poems*, trans. Brenda Walker. Damascus: Dar Talas, 1984.

Janabi, Hatif, *Questions and their Retinue: Selected Poems*, trans. Khaled Mattawa. Fayetteville, AR: University of Arkansas Press, 1996.

Juwaydah, Faruq, *Had We Not Parted*, trans. Muhammad Enani. Cairo: GEBO, 1999.

—— *A Thousand Faces Has the Moon*, trans. Muhammad Enani. Cairo: GEBO, 1997.

Kabbani, Nizar, see Qabbani.

Kashghari, Badia [Badi'ah], *The Unattainable Lotus*, trans. by the author. London: Saqi, 2001.

al-Maghut, Muhammad, *The Fans of Swords: Poems*, trans. May Jayyusi and Naomi Shihab Nye. Washington, DC: Three Continents Press, 1991.

—— *Joy Is Not my Profession*, trans. John Asfour and Alison Burch. Montreal: Signal Editions, 1994.

Mahdi, Sami, *Poems*, trans. Mohammad Darwish. Baghdad: Dar al-Ma'mun, 1988.

Matar, Muhammad Afifi, *Quartet of Joy: Poems*, trans. Ferial Ghazoul and John Verlenden. Fayetteville, AR: University of Arkansas Press, 1997.

Mikhail, Dunya, *Diary of a Wave outside the Sea*, trans. by the author and ed. by Louise I Hartung. Cairo: Ishtar Publishing House, 1999.

Muhammadi, Habibah, *Time in the Wilderness*, trans. Muhammad Inani [Enani]. Cairo: GEBO, 2000.

Naimy, Nadeem, see Hawi, Khalil.

Qabbani, Nizar, *Arabian Love Poems*, trans. Bassam K. Frangieh and Clementina Brown. Colorado Springs, CO: Three Continents Press, 1993.

—— *On Entering the Sea: The Erotic and Other Poetry of Nizar Qabbani*, trans. Lena Jayyusi and Sharif Elmusa with Jack Collom et al. New York: Interlink Books, 1996.

—— *Poems of Love and Exile* [Min qasa'id al-'ishq wa al-manfa], trans. Saadun Suayeh [Sa'dun Suwayyih]. Beirut: Dar Sadir, 1998.

—— *Republic of Love: Selected Poems*, trans. Nayef al-Kalali. London: Kegan Paul International, 2000.

Qurashi, Hasan Abd Allah, *Specters of Exile and Other Poems*, trans. John Heath-Stubbs and Catherine Cobhan. London: Echoes, 1991.

al-Qusaybi, Ghazi, *From the Orient and the Desert* London: Kegan Paul, 1977, 1994; Stocksfield, UK: Oriel Press, 1979.

—— *Dusting the Colour from Roses: A Bilingual Anthology of Arabic Poetry*, trans. A. A. Ruffai. Revised by Heather Lawton. London: Echoes, 1995.

Sa'adeh, Wadih, *A Secret Sky*, transcreated from the Arabic by Anne Fairbairn. Charnwood, Australia: Ginninderra Press, 1997.

al-Sabah, Su'ad Mubarak, *Fragments of a Woman*, trans. Nehad Selaiha. Cairo: GEBO, 1990.

—— *In the Beginning Was the Female*, trans. Abdul Wahid Lu'lu'a. Beirut: Dar Sadir, 1994.

Sa'd, Maryam Qasim, *A Handful of Earth: Selected Poems* London: Aurora Press, 1993.

Sa'id, Hamid, *Poems*, trans. Salman al-Wasiti. Baghdad: Dar al-Ma'mun, 1988.

Salim, Umar, *Ghana Reveals her Secrets*, trans. Gibrill al-Munir, Accra, Ghana: Unity Media Ventures, 2002 [Lybia].

al-Saqlawi, Sa'id, *The Awakening of the Moon: A Selection of Poems*, trans. Abdullah al-Shahham and M. V. McDonald. Muscat, Oman: al-Batinah Publishing Co., 1996.

Saudi, Mona [Muna], *An Ocean of Dreams: Forty-Three Poems*, trans. Tania Tamari Nasir. Pueblo, CO: Passeggiata Press, 1999.

al-Sayyab, Badr Shakir, *Selected Poems*, trans. Nadia Bishai. London: Third World Centre for Research and Publishing, 1986. Reissued without reference to this edition, Cairo: GEBO, 2001.

al-Shabbi, Abu al-Qasim, *Songs of Life: Selections from the Poetry of Abu'l Qasim al-Shabbi*, trans. Lena Jayyusi and Naomi Shihab Nye. Carthage, Tunisia: National Foundation for Translation, 1987.

Shusha, Faruq, *The Language of Lovers' Blood*, trans. Muhammad Enani. Cairo: GEBO, 1999.

—— *Time to Catch Time*, trans. Muhammad Enani. Cairo: GEBO, 1997.

al-Suwaydi, Muhammad Ahmad, *Pathways of Dawn*, trans. Zaki Anwar Nusseibeh. Abu Dhabi, UAE: n. p., 1997.

al-Tall, Mustafa Wahbi, *Mustafa's Journey: Verse of Arar, Poet of Jordan*, trans. Richard Loring Taylor. Irbid, Jordan: Yarmouk University, 1988.

—— *Arar: The Poet and Lover of Jordan*. Selected by Abdullah Radwan and trans. Sadik I. Odeh. Amman: Greater Amman Municipality Celebrations of Arar's Birthday 100th Anniversary, 1999 [Includes selected poems: 93–166].

Tuqan, Fadwa, *Daily Nightmares: Ten Poems*, trans. Yusra A. Salah. New York: Vantage Press, 1988; [S. I.]: The Palestinian Writers' Union, 1991.

—— 'Poems', trans. Naomi Shihab Nye. In Tuqan's *A Mountainous Journey: An Autobiography*, trans. Olive Kenny. London: The Women's Press, 1990: 206–239.

—— *Selected Poems of Fadwa Tuqan*, trans. Ibrahim Dawood. Irbid, Jordan: Yarmouk University, 1994.

Yusuf, Sa'di [also known as Youssef, Saadi], *Without an Alphabet, Without a Map*, trans. Khaled Mattawa. St Paul, MN: Graywolf Press, 2002.

—— *Troubled Waters*, Poems, Beirut: Dar al-Mada Publishers, 1995. According to the poet, this collection includes translations by Ferial Zaghloul, Fawwaz Trabulsi and Abdullah al-Udhari].

Zoghaib, Henri, *In Forbidden Time: Love Poems*, trans. Adnan Haydar and Michael Beard. Washington, DC: New Pen Bond Publishers, 1991.

CHAPTER FIVE

Arabic Poetry in International Anthologies: A Partial but Positive Representation

The bibliography below reflects what I consider to be the third phase of the representation in English that modern Arabic poetry has attained in recent decades. We have already seen the increased visibility of Arabic poetry as a result, first, of the countless poems that have appeared and continue to appear in numerous English literary journals, and second, of the fairly large number of anthologies or collections that have become accessible. The latter, published in both Arabic- and English-speaking countries, vary in their literary quality, their representation or scope and the criteria and methods by which they were collected or translated. As classified earlier, they include (1) Pan-Arab anthologies, (2) country or region-related anthologies or collections (Arabia, Egypt, Iraq, Jordan, Kuwait, Morocco, UAE and Yemen) and (3) works of individual poets from different Arab countries anthologies.

Admittedly, not all published collections or anthologies (which number thus far more than eighty) can be regarded as representing the finest trends in modern Arabic poetry or the remarkable achievements of many Arab poets. Indeed, one may raise serious questions about the literary quality of certain works, whether they are judged on the basis of their original Arabic or their translated versions. Nonetheless, viewed *in toto*, they provide us with many poems, which illustrate the vitality, modernity and thematic richness of contemporary Arabic poetry. This is especially evident in poems that have been rendered into English by noted American, British, Irish and other English-speaking poets such as Alan Brownjohn, Samuel Hazo, John Heath-Stubbs, W. S. Merwin, Desmond O'Grady and Richard Wilbur.[1] In short, contemporary Arabic poetry is currently represented by a good number of

---

1. Note the list of second translators in *Modern Arabic Poetry: An Anthology*, ed. Salma Khadra Jayyusi. New York: Columbia University Press, 1987: 494–498.

poems that are likely to appeal not only to students of Arabic literature but also to readers of world poetry in general.

The way in which Arabic poetry is represented in world anthologies has been rarely discussed, in spite of its relevance to the West's reception of modern Arabic literature. A more thorough and detailed examination of this question is needed for several reasons. Such anthologies have, to paraphrase Rainer Schulte's remarks[1] on a related subject, an important function in the transfer of poets from other countries into the English-speaking world (Schulte, 1995: 136). Widely used by readers in both academic and non-academic contexts, anthologies or specialized collections of international poetry serve to promote, in one volume, a general awareness of other literary traditions and an appreciation of the experiences or concerns revealed in the works of different international poets. They may also engender in certain cases a sustained interest in studying or translating a particular national literature or a poet. Indeed, some anthologists consider sending 'readers to the original' as a primary purpose of editing anthologies of world poetry. In addition, such anthologies may shed light on the place of different national poets (such as Arab poets) in relation to major trends, issues and practices in world poetry or the literary taste prevalent among readers and editors/ anthologists in the target languages.

In addressing this question, I have referred briefly (1985) to *al-hisar al-adabi* (the literary siege, or embargo),[2] which modern Arabic poetry continued to experience in the West or, more specifically, in the United States and other English-speaking countries. A survey of English anthologies or selections of world poetry published before 1985 revealed at that time a widespread tendency to exclude Arabic poetry, with the notable exception of works covering women's poetry. (Note, for example, unmarked items in the bibliography below.) A similar pattern was evident in other general reference works, which completely overlooked or marginalized Arabic poetry. Consider, for example, Magill's *Critical Survey of Poetry: Foreign Languages Series* (1984),

---

1. Rainer Schulte. 'International Literature Transfer via Translation Anthologies', *International Anthologies of Literature in Translation*, ed. Harald Kittel. Berlin: Erich Schmidt Verlag, 1995: 134–148.

2. Salih J. Altoma, 'Mulahazat hawl tarjamat al-shi'r al-'arabi al-hadith wa makanatih fi al-gharb', *al-Bayan* Kuwait (January 1986): 150–165.

—— 'al-Shi'r al-'arabi al-mutarjam: makanatuh fi al-shi'r al-'alami wa harakat al-tarjama al-mu'asira', *Makanat al-shi'r fi al-thaqafa al-'arabiyya al-mu'asira* Baghdad: Ministry of Culture, 1987: 23–41.

—— *Modern Arabic Poetry in English Translation: A Bibliography* Tangier: The King Fahd School of Translation, 1993. See especially the Arabic section pp. 1–28, and the English section, p. 7 and pp. 11–13, 'Anthologies of World Poetry in English Translation'.

whose stated ' mission' was 'to survey briefly the creative works of significant poets whose means of verbal expression is non-English'. What the five volumes of the survey cover in reality is mostly poets from Western languages: Catalan, Czechoslovakian, German, French, Ancient and modern Greek, Hungarian, Italian, Latin, Polish, Russian, Spanish and the Scandinavian and Yugoslav languages. Other non-Western traditions or languages surveyed include Chinese, Indian–English poetry, Japanese, Third World poetry and Tibetan, in addition to Omar Khayyam and Sa'di as representative of 'Ancient Persia'. If there is any reference to Arabic poetry, it was made in connection with Omar Khayyam, who, we are told, wrote poems in Arabic also.

However, the pattern began to change in the late 1980s, as more anthologies and relevant reference works sought to incorporate selections from Arabic and other developing countries' literature. Several factors have produced this significant shift towards a wider representation of Arabic and other previously marginalized literature. The first, as we have noted above, is the global recognition that Arabic literature began to receive when Najib Mahfuz was awarded the Nobel Prize for Literature. The second is the proliferation of highly successful translations or anthologies of Arabic poetry, as noted above. Other factors include the contribution that post-colonial, multicultural and women's studies have made to representing other cultures and Edward Said's persistent and influential efforts against bias in this field.

The bibliography below includes different types of anthologies or collections with equally different objectives in mind: academic and non-academic, theme-, subject- or period-oriented, and more universal or general. The first obvious observation is with regard to the greater representation of modern Arabic poetry in English anthologies of international/world poetry, as indicated by asterisks (*). Nevertheless, the question arises over the choice or omission of particular poets or poems. Forbes's monumental and laudable anthology of the twentieth century in poetry includes, for example, only Mahmud Darwish in a section entitled 'Lost Tribes: the Middle East 1948–'. The section itself presents more poems by three other poets, Yehuda Amichai, James Fenton and Jon Silken. Forbes's choice was obviously dictated by the calamitous nature of the Palestinian/Arab–Israeli conflict, but, by limiting himself to this conflict, Forbes overlooked other catastrophic events or wars in the Arab world, which many Arab poets such as Adonis or Sa'di Yusuf have addressed in their poetry. This is not to mention the section's exclusion of other Palestinian poets such as Fadwa Tuqan. McClatchy, a highly regarded poet–critic, seems to have aimed at allocating equal space to both Arab and Israeli poets in his anthology *The Vintage Book of Contemporary World Poetry* (1996). His selections include twelve poems by two Arab poets (Adonis and Darwish) and eighteen poems by three Israeli poets. McClatchy thus fails to achieve a broader or more balanced representation of poets from different parts of the Arab world including in particular Egypt, Iraq, Lebanon and Morocco.

In my view, the most regrettable case of omission is *World Poetry: An Anthology of Verse from Antiquity to our Time* (1998) edited by Katharine Washburn et al. The anthology stands out as the most comprehensive, informative and remarkable attempt we have seen in recent years. It gathers in one volume (1,338 pp.) 'the universe of verse', a 4,000-year period, 1,600 poems and dozens of languages including Classical Arabic. The anthology has been acclaimed rightly by many critics and characterized as 'enduring', 'indispensable' and 'the first of its kind with fresh translations', etc. It is noted for its representation of numerous modern poets writing in 'non-European languages' such as Bengali, Chinese, Hindi, Indonesian, Japanese, Korean, Lao, Marathi, Tamil, Turkish, Urdu and Vietnamese.

Hebrew is also represented, not in association with the other non-European languages, but within a European context, in the section entitled 'Poetry in the Languages of Continental Europe'. This unconventional classification of Hebrew is due perhaps to the fact that the three Hebrew/Israeli poets who were chosen for the anthology were born in the West: Yehuda Amichai (Würzburg, Germany), T. Carmi (New York) and Dan Pagis (Bukovina, Romania). As for Arabic or the Arab world, the anthology completely leaves out modern Arabic poetry, for inexplicable reasons.

Even the note on the section 'The Twentieth Century 1915–' glosses over the Arab world in its reference to 'anti-imperial and anticolonial movements' in different regions of the non-Western world: China, Indonesia, Turkey and Africa.[1] To overlook Arabic and the Arab world, is most perplexing, as Arabic is a major world language and heir to one of the longest continuous literary traditions, and the Arab world has been in a state of constant contact or confrontation with Europe for many centuries. It is of course possible to attribute such an omission to one or more of the familiar reasons: bias or prejudice, lack of knowledge about recent translations from Arabic, questions about the literary value of the translations themselves, the notion that modern Arabic poetry is well represented in other anthologies or the rationalization that not all national literatures can be represented, and that omission of one sort or another is unavoidable. However, no reason can be adduced to justify the complete exclusion of modern Arabic poetry in an anthology of this extraordinary range. I should add that the anthology does include a few French

---

1. See Washburn's anthology p. 891. The coeditor, John S. Major, wrote the note.

poems by Egyptian and Algerian poets: Andrée Chedid, Joyce Mansour and Malika O'Lahsen.[1]

As the annotated bibliography below indicates, similar questions can be raised about the exclusion of Arabic poetry or its limited or partial representation in other anthologies. Nevertheless, the bibliography provides ample evidence of the greater visibility and representation Arabic poetry has gained in recent years.

Arabic Poetry and International Anthologies: A Bibliography

The entries that include selections from the works of modern Arab poets are marked by *

*Aharoni, Ada et al., eds, *A Song to Life and World Peace: Selected Essays and Poems Presented at the XIII World Congress of Poets of the World Academy of Arts and Culture* Jerusalem: Posner & Sons, 1993 [Includes a single poem, 'Usual View' by Fawaz Hussein, 'translated from Arabic into Hebrew by the poet, and into English by Ada Aharoni.' Only the Hebrew and English versions are given (125)].

---

1. Elizabeth Washburn (d. 2000), a noted poet, translator, essayist and editor, was responsible for the selection of poetry from a large area including the Near East. She states in her introduction: 'My own territory encompassed the poetry of our own language from both the British Isles and America, the work of the West from Mesopotamia, Egypt, and the classical world through contemporary Europe in both Western and Eastern European languages, and, because the links are arguably so strong between Europe and the Near East, the poetry of two Semitic languages – Hebrew and Arabic – and Persian.' (Washburn xviii–xix)

   It was with Washburn's statement in mind that I wrote a letter to her (October 8, 1999) seeking her clarification on the exclusion of modern Arabic poetry. I said in my letter that, 'some progress has been made in recent years toward ensuring more successful translation of modern Arabic poems thanks to the participation of English-speaking poets (American and others). Note, for example, Samuel Hazo's translations of Adonis and Jayyusi's *Modern Arabic Poetry* (Columbia University Press, 1987). I am wondering whether you have had a chance to review such translations or you were unable to select for your anthology any of the Arabic poems to which you had access. I would greatly appreciate your comment or views regarding this matter.' Washburn was kind enough to respond by e-mail in a message dated December 23, 1999: 'I just returned (yesterday) from three months in Ireland and Rome, where the email reception was not all I'd hoped for – and discovered, much to my dismay, your letter among many other strayed messages. Do bear with me a bit longer, and I'll respond to your interesting and thoughtful letter in more detail. In the meantime, best wishes and a happy new year.' That was unfortunately the only and last response I received from Washburn, a few months before her untimely death on March 22, 2000.

*Arkin, Marian, and Barbara Shollar, eds, *Longman Anthology of World Literature by Women, 1875–1975* New York: Longman, 1989 [Includes Malak Abd al-Aziz, 'We Asked' and 'The Fall'; Fawziyya Abu Khalid, 'Tattoo Writing' and 'Mother's Inheritance'; Zabyah Khamis, 'From Fading of Memory' and 'The Ten Commandments'; Nazik al-Mala'ikah, 'I Am', 'Washing Off Disgrace' and 'Jamila' (in addition to an excerpt from her book *Issues of Contemporary Poetry*); and Fadwa Tuqan, 'After the Release', 'The Last Knocks', 'Nothing Is Here' and 'To Etan'].

*Atwan, Robert, George Dardess and Peggy Rosenthal, eds, *Divine Inspiration: The Life of Jesus in World Poetry* New York: Oxford University Press, 1998 [Includes Khalil Hawi, 'The Magi in Europe'; Jabra I. Jabra, 'A Stranger at the Fountain'; Yusuf al-Khal, 'The Eternal Dialogue' and 'Repentance'; Tawfiq Sayigh, 'The Sermon on the Mount'; Badr Shakir al-Sayyab, 'City of Sinbad' and 'The Messiah After the Crucifixion'; and Fadwa Tuqan, 'To Christ'].

*Baird, Vanessa, ed., *Eye to Eye, Women: Their Words and their Worlds* Oxford, UK: New Internationalist, 1996; London; New York: Serpent's Tail, 1997; Toronto, Ont.: Second Story Press, 1997, 1996 [Malak Abd al-Aziz, 'The Fall'].

*Bankier, Joanna, and Deirdre Lashgari, eds, *Women Poets of the World* New York: Macmillan, 1983 [Includes Fawziyya Abu Khalid, 'Mother's Inheritance'; Nazik al-Mala'ikah, 'Jamila'; Mona Sa'udi, 'When the Loneliness of the Tomb', 'How Do I Enter the Silence of Stones' and 'Why Don't I Write in the Language of the Air?'; and Fadwa Tuqan, from 'Behind the Bars'. This is in addition to Arabic poems by pre-modern poets and poems written originally in French or English by three modern poets: Evelyn Accad, Etel Adnan and Andrée Chedid].

*Bankier, Joanna, et al., eds, *The Other Voice: Twentieth Century Women's Poetry in English Translation* New York: Norton, 1976 [Includes Nazik al-Mala'ikah, 'Elegy for a Woman of No Importance'; Saniya Salih, 'Exile'; Fadwa Tuqan, from 'Behind the Bars I'; in addition to Etel Adnan, Venus Khoury and Nadia Tueni].

*Barnstone, Willis, and Tony Barnstone, eds, *Literatures of Asia, Africa, and Latin America* Upper Saddle River, NJ: Prentice Hall, 1999 [Includes Adonis, from 'The Desert'; Mahmud Darwish, 'The Prison Cell' and 'Victim No. 48'; Hatif Janabi, 'Questions and their Retinue'; Badr Shakir al-Sayyab, 'Song in August'; and Nizar Qabbani, 'Bread, Hashish, and Moon'].

Barnstone, Aliki, and Willis Barnstone, eds, *A Book of Women Poets from Antiquity to Now* New York: Schocken, 1980. Revised Edition, 1992

[Includes pre-modern poems and poems written in French by Andrée Chedid (b. 1921), Venus Khoury (b. 1937) and Nadia Tueni (b. 1935)].

Bates, Scott, ed., *Poems of War Resistance from 2300 BC to the Present* New York: Grossman, 1969.

Benedikt, Michael, ed., *The Prose Poem: An International Anthology* New York: Dell, 1976 [Apart from a few Japanese prose poems, the anthology represents the genre in Western languages].

*Bernstein, Charles, ed., *99 Poets/1999: An International Poetics Symposium* A special issue of *Boundary 2* 26 (Summer 1999) [An anthology of international responses to questions on poetry. It includes statements by six Arab poets: Adonis (Syria/Lebanon), Mahmud Darwish (Palestine), Abdellatif Laabi (Morocco), Abdelwahab Meddeb (Tunisia), Amina Said (Tunisia) and Habib Tengour (Algeria)].

*Biddle, Arthur W., et al., eds, *Global Voices: Contemporary Literature from the Non-Western World* Englewood Cliffs, NJ: Prentice Hall, 1995 [Includes only two Arab poets: from Kuwait, Su'ad al-Mubarak al-Sabah, 'Third World', 'A Thousand Times More Beautiful', 'A Covenant', 'Sojourn Forever', 'Free Harbour' and 'You Alone'; and from Iraq, Badr Shakir al-Sayyab, 'Rain Song' and 'Song in August'].

Bly, Robert, ed., *News of the Universe: Poems of Twofold Consciousness* San Francisco: Sierra Club Books, 1980.

—— *The Soul Is Here for its Own Joy: Sacred Poems from Many Cultures* Hopewell, NJ: The Ecco Press, 1995 [Two poems by pre-modern poets: Ibn Faraj, 'Chastity' from *Poems of Arab Andalusia*, translated by Cola Franzen from the Spanish version of Emilio Garcia Gomez (San Francisco: City Lights Books, 1989); and Ibn Hazm, 'Separation by Death' adapted by Robert Bly from the translation of Alois Richard Nykl, from *The Sea and Honeycomb*, edited by Robert Bly (Madison, MI: Sixties Press, 1966)].

*Boothe, Wayne, *The Art of Growing Older: Writers on Living and Aging*, ed. Wayne Boothe. Chicago: University of Chicago Press, 1992 [Includes Buland al-Haydari, 'Old Age', and Yusuf al-Khal, 'Old Age'].

*Bould, Geoffrey, ed., *Conscience Be my Guide: An Anthology of Prison Writings* London: Zed Books, 1991 [Includes Nabil Janabi, 'Those Words I Said', and Abdellatif Laabi, 'A Long Way to Cherry Time'].

Buck, Philo Melvin, ed., *An Anthology of World Literature* Third edition. New York: Macmillan, 1951 [Includes four short lyrics from earlier periods and extracts from the Qur'an].

*Clerk, Jayana, and Ruth Siegel, eds, *Modern Literature of the Non-Western World: Where the Waters Are Born* New York: HarperCollins College Publishers,

1995 [Includes Fawziyya Abu Khalid, 'A Pearl'; Abdullah al-Baradduni, 'Answers to One Question'; Mahmud Darwish, 'Guests of the Sea'; Abd al-Aziz al-Maqalih, 'Sanaa Is Hungry'; Fadwa Tuqan, 'Song of Becoming'; in addition to texts written originally in English by Khalil Gibran, 'On Children'; and Etel Adnan, 'In the Heart of the Heart of Another Country'].

*Chipasula, Stella, and Frank Chipasula, eds, *The Heinemann Book of African Women's Poetry* London: Heinemann, 1995 [Includes Malak Abd al-Aziz, 'We Asked' and 'The Fall', and other Francophone poets from Algeria, Egypt, Morocco and Tunisia. This is in contrast to Moore's anthology of modern African poetry; see below].

Cohen, J. M., ed., *The Rider Book of Mystical Verse* London: Hutchinson, 1982 [Includes al-Hallaj (d. 922) and al-Ma'arri (d. 1057)].

*Cosman, Carol, Joan Keefe and Kathleen Weaver, eds, *The Penguin Book of Women Poets* New York: Viking Press, c. 1978, 1979, 1988 [Includes Samar Attar, from 'The Return of the Dead'; Fadwa Tuqan, 'After Twenty Years'; Nadia Tueni, who writes in French; and al-Khansa' and Walladah from the classical period].

Engle, Paul, et al., eds, *The World Comes to Iowa: Iowa International Anthology* Ames, IA: Iowa State University Press, 1987.

Ferlinghetti, Lawrence, ed., *City Lights Pocket Poets Anthology* San Francisco, CA: City Lights Books, 1995 [Based on forty years of City Lights Pocket Poets – fifty-two volumes – the anthology includes American, European and Latin American poets who reflect, according to the editor, 'an international, dissident, insurgent ferment'].

*Flattley, Kerry, and Chris Wallace-Crabe, eds, *From the Republic of Conscience: An International Anthology of Poetry* Flemington, Victoria, Australia: Aird Books, 1992; New York: White Pine Press, 1993 [Includes Sa'di Yusuf, 'Hamra Night'; Muhammad al-Maghut, 'The Postman's Fear'; and Mahmud Darwish, 'I Have Witnessed the Massacre'].

*Forbes, Peter, ed., *Scanning the Century: The Penguin Book of the Twentieth Century in Poetry* London: Viking, in Association with The Poetry Society, 1999 [Includes Mahmud Darwish, from 'Beirut' and 'We Travel Like Other People'].

*Forche, Carolyn, ed., *Against Forgetting: Twentieth-Century Poetry of Witness* New York: Norton, 1993 [Includes Adonis, 'The New Noah', 'Elegy for the Time at Hand' and 'A Mirror for the Twentieth Century'; Mahmud Darwish, 'Earth Poem', 'We Travel Like Other People', 'Prison' and 'Psalm

2'; and Fadwa Tuqan, 'Face Lost in the Wilderness', 'After Twenty Years', 'I Won't Sell his Love', 'Behind the Bars, Sel' and 'Song of Becoming'].

Friebert, Stuart, and David Young, eds, *Models of the Universe: An Anthology of Prose Poem* Oberlin: Oberlin College Press, 1995 [An anthology representing about two centuries of the prose poem in Western languages, in spite of the reference in the introduction (20) to 'the process of identifying and choosing prose poems from all over the world'].

Garrigue, Jean, ed., *Translations by American Poets* Athens, OH: Ohio University Press, 1970 [Translations by forty-six American poets of poems from Japanese and ten Western languages].

*Hamalian, Leo, and John D. Yohannan, eds, *New Writing From the Middle East*. A Mentor Book. New York: New American Library, 1978 [Includes Salah Abd al-Sabur, 'The Tartars Have Struck' and 'People in My Country'; Adonis, 'The Frontiers of Despair', 'You Have No Choice', 'The City' and 'A Mirror for Autumn'; Abd al-Wahhab al-Bayati, 'Why Are We in Exile, the Refugees Ask' and 'The Wall'; Mahmud Darwish, 'Pride and Fury'; Buland al-Haidari [Haydari], 'The Dead Witness' and 'The Parcel'; Rashid Husain [Husayn], 'Lessons in Parsing'; Jabra Ibrahim Jabra, 'In the Deserts of Exile'; Nizar Qabbani, 'Comments on the Notebook of Decadence', 'Bread, Hashish, and Moon', 'I Am the Train of Sadness' and 'A Personal Letter to the Month of June'; Tawfiq Sayigh, 'The Sermon on the Mount' and Badr Shakir al-Sayyab, 'For I Am a Stranger' and 'Burning'].

Hamill, Sam, ed., *The Gift of Tongues: Twenty-Five Years from Copper Canyon Press* Port Townsend, WA: Copper Canyon Press, 1996.

*Hampl, Patricia, ed., *Burning Bright: An Anthology of Sacred Poetry* New York: Ballantine Books, 1995 [Includes Gibran Khalil Gibran, 'The Seven Stages'; Nazik al-Mala'ikah, 'Song for the Moon'; Orkhan Muyassar, 'Lost'; Huda Na'mani, 'Love Poem'; Amjad Nasir, 'Loneliness'; Fu'ad Rifqa, 'The Fortune Teller'; Ahmad Shawqi, 'An Andalusian Exile'; Fadwa Tuqan, 'I Found it'; and Ahmad al-Udwani, from 'Signs'].

Hirshfield, Jane, ed., *Women in Praise of the Sacred: 43 Centuries of Spiritual Poetry by Women* New York: HarperCollins, 1994 [Includes only Rabi'a al-Adawiyya from the classical period].

Jay, Peter, ed., *The Spaces of Hope: Poetry for our Times and Places* London: Anvil Press Poetry, 1998 [With two exceptions, the poems are selected from Anvil Press Poetry publications 1969–98. They include translations primarily from Western and Chinese languages].

*Jones, Richard, ed., *The Last Believer in Words: An Anthology of Poems in Translation from the Pages of* Poetry East. A special issue of *Poetry East* (45–46 [1998]) [Includes Mahmud Darwish, 'I Am From There'].

Junkins, Donald, ed., *The Contemporary World Poets* New York: Harcourt, 1976 [Includes only poems by Mohammed Dib, a noted Algerian Francophone writer].

*Kharrat, Edward, and Nihad Salem, eds, *Afro-Asian Poetry: An Anthology* Cairo: Atlas Press, 1971 [Includes Jili Abd al-Rahman, 'The Street Is Shaking O'Lorca' and 'The Two Mates on the Banks of Remembrance'; Salah Abd al-Sabur, 'The Hanging of Zahran' and 'The Tartars Have Struck'; Muhammad Abu Sinna, 'Eternal Egypt'; Adonis, 'Chapter of An Old Image' and 'The One Who Left before Time'; Abd al-Wahhab al-Bayati, 'al-Hallaj's Agony' and 'The Descent of Orpheus'; Mu'in Basisu, 'The Island of Ancient Mottoes' and 'The Lamp and the Mill'; Mahmud Darwish, 'The Martyr of a Song', 'A Lover from Palestine' and 'The Man with the Green Shadow'; Amal Dunqul, 'The Last Supper'; Muhammad al-Fituri, 'He Died Tomorrow'; Taj al-Sirr al-Hasan, 'Going on the Pilgrimage'; Ahmad Abd al-Mu'ti Hijazi, 'Blood of Lumumba'; Mahmud Hasan Isma'il, 'Self and Sin'; Salih Jawdat, 'The Dark Star'; Nazih Khayr, 'Illusion'; Muhammad Mahjub, 'Little Adam'; Nazik al-Mala'ikah, 'The Top of the Stairs'; Muhammad Afifi Matar, 'Of the Moon of Summer and of Man'; Abd al-Karim al-Na'im, 'Our Cause and the Discovery of the Moon'; Samih al-Qasim, 'To All the Smartly Dressed Men in the UN'; Radi Sadduq, 'A Song of a Revolutionary without Identity'; Badr Shakir al-Sayyab, 'In Front of the Gate of Allah'; Shadhil Taqah, 'And the Man Returned'; and Tawfiq Zayyad, 'Bury Your Dead and Rise'].

*Kritzeck, James, ed., *Modern Islamic Literature from 1800 to the Present* New York: Holt, Rinehart and Winston, 1970 [Includes Ahmad Zaki Abu Shadi, 'The Maiden of Bekhten'; Abbas Mahmud al-Aqqad, 'Untitled', 'Love's Companion', 'Competition' and 'Cheat Me!'; Abd al-Majid Ibn Jallun, 'Who Art Thou?'; Ma'ruf al-Rusafi, 'Sleepers, Wake!'; Abu al-Qasim al-Shabbi, 'Untitled' [extract from 'The Will to Live']; Ahmad Shawqi, 'To a Late Composer'; and Khayr al-Din al-Zirikli, 'Lament'].

*Langer, Jennifer, ed., *The Bend in the Road: Refugees Writing* Nottingham, UK: Five Leaves Publications, 1997 [Includes Sargoun Boulus, 'My Father's Dream'; Buland al-Haydari, 'Conversation at the Bend in the Road'; Fawzi Karim, 'The Dawn Is Imminent'; Abd al-Karim Kassid, 'The King and the Shoes' and Sadiq al-Sayigh, 'Spectacle'].

Linthwaite, Illona, ed., *Ain't I a Woman: A Book of Women's Poetry from around the World* New York: P. Bedrick Books, 1988 [A collection of 150 poems from around the world intended to redress the omission of women's works in traditional anthologies. It includes Mririda n'Ait Attik, a Berber poet–singer from Morocco].

*Lomax, Alan, and Raoul Abdul, eds, *Three Thousand Years of Black Poetry* New York: Dodd, Mead, 1970; Second edition 1984 [Includes Muhammad al-Fituri, 'The Knell' and 'I Am a Negro' and Salah Jahine, 'Quatrains,' in addition to other pre-modern poets].

*Lowenfels, Walter, ed., *For Neruda, for Chile: An International Anthology* Boston: Beacon Press, 1975 [Includes Yusuf al-Khal, 'For Neruda upon his Death' and Etel Adnan, 'A Candle for Pablo Neruda'].

*McClatchy, J. D., ed., *The Vintage Book of Contemporary World Poetry* New York: Vintage Books, 1996 [Includes four poems by Adonis: 'The Passage', 'Tree of Fire', 'Song of a Man in the Dark' and 'Elegy for the Time at Hand'; and eight poems by Mahmud Darwish: 'Identity Card', 'On Wishes', 'Victim Number 48', 'Steps in the Night', 'We Walk towards a Land', 'Sirhan Drinks his Coffee in the Cafeteria', 'Words' and 'Guests on the Sea'. See 285–307 for twelve Arabic poems and 308–336 for eighteen Hebrew poems by three poets].

McGreal, Ian, ed., *Great Literature of the Eastern World* New York: HarperCollins, 1996 [Includes 'descriptive essays on over 100 of the most noteworthy literary works of China, India, Japan, Korea, and the Middle East' (ix). The section on Arabic literature covers largely works from the classical period (including the Seven Pre-Islamic Odes, the Qur'an, and the *Arabian Nights*) in addition to three modern writers: Taha Husayn, Tawfiq al-Hakim and Ghassan Kanafani].

Magil, Frank N., ed., *Critical Survey of Poetry: Foreign Languages Series* 5 vols. Englewood Cliffs, NJ: Salem Press, 1984 [Covers Catalan, Chinese, Czechoslovakian, German, French, Ancient and modern Greek, Hungarian, Indian–English, Italian, Japanese, Latin, Polish, Russian, Scandinavian, Spanish, Third World, Tibetan and Yugoslavian poetry].

Merwin, W. S., *Selected Translations: 1948–1968* New York: Atheneum, 1968.

—— *Selected Translations: 1968–1978* New York: Atheneum, 1979.

Milosz, Czeslaw, ed., *A Book of Luminous Things: An International Anthology of Poetry* New York: Harcourt Brace and Co., 1996.

Mitchell, Stephen, ed., *The Enlightened Heart: An Anthology of Sacred Poetry* New York: HarperPerennial, 1989.

Moore, Gerald, and Ulli Beier, eds, *The Penguin Book of Modern African Poetry* Third edition. Harmondsworth, UK: Penguin Books, 1984 [Excludes

Arabic poetry of North African countries, in contrast to Chipasula's anthology of African women's poetry listed above].

Murray, Joan, ed., *Poems to Live by in Uncertain Times* Boston, MA: Beacon Press, 2001 [Includes the translation of 'Return to the Village' written originally in Hebrew by Na'im Araidi, an Arab–Israeli poet].

*New World Writing: Fifth Mentor Selection New York: The New American Library of World Literature, 1954 [Includes four modern Arabic poems selected and translated by Desmond Stewart: Buland al-Haydari, 'Sterility' and 'Arrogance'; Muhammad Qasim, 'To a Basketball Player'; and Ibrahim Tuqan, 'The Doves'].

**Nye, Naomi Shihab, ed., *This Same Sky: A Collection of Poems from around the World* New York: Four Winds Press, 1992 [An anthology of 129 poets from sixty-two countries, selected for young readers. It includes Fawziyya Abu Khalid, 'Distances of Longing' and 'A Pearl'; Salim Barakat, 'The Squirrel'; Ali Darwish, 'Or'; Mahmud Darwish, 'The Prison Cell'; Muhammad al-Fayiz, 'A Sailor's Memoirs'; Muhammad al-Ghuzzi, 'The Pen'; Muhammad al-Maghut, 'The Orphan'; Ali al-Mak, 'The Gatherer'; Fuad Rifqa, from 'A Diary of a Woodcutter'; Yusuf al-Sayigh, 'Ants'; Nadia Tueni, 'In the Lebanese Mountains'; and Fadwa Tuqan, 'Between Ebb and Flow'].

**—— *The Space Between Our Footsteps: Poems and Paintings from the Middle East* New York: Simon & Schuster, 1998 [Prepared as a book for young readers, the collection includes poems by Adonis, Joseph Abi Dahir, Shawqi Abi Shaqra, Fawziyya Abu Khalid, Mahmud Adwan, Kaisar Afif, Layla Allush, Sa'id Aql, Muhammad al-As'ad, Fawzi al-Asmar, Salim Barakat, Abd al-Wahhab al-Bayati, Mahmud Darwish, Zuhur Dixson, Salah Fa'iq, Muhammad al-Ghuzzi, Qasim Haddad, Muhammad Afif Husayni, Hatif Janabi, Ali al-Jundi, Shafiq al-Kamali, Yusuf al-Khal, Ahmad Muhammad al-Khalifa, Dhabiya Khamis, Sami Mahdi, Muhammad al-Qasi, Samih al-Qasim, Abd al-Rahim Salih al-Rahim, Fu'ad Rifqa, Mona al-Sa'udi, Abu al-Qasim al-Shabbi, Hashim Shafiq, Mahmud Shurayh, Fadwa Tuqan and Sa'di Yusuf].

**O'Grady, Desmond, *Trawling Tradition: Translations 1954–1994* Salzburg: University of Salzburg, 1994 [Includes The Seven Pre-Islamic Odes, three poems by Abu Nuwas (d. 810?) and thirty-two poems from the works of ten modern Arab poets: Ahmad Shawqi, 'In Exile', 'Bois de Boulogne' and 'Thoughts on School Children'; Ilya Abu Madi, 'Human Clay', 'The Phoenix', 'Philosophy of Life' and 'In the Wilderness'; Ibrahim Naji, 'Fake Hopes', 'Oblivion', 'Farewell', 'The Stranger' and 'The Return'; Ibrahim Tuqan, 'The Commando' and 'The Martyr'; Badawi al-Jabal, 'Beauty', 'The

Visit', 'Immortality' and 'Poem to God'; Yusuf Bashir al-Tijani, 'My Village School', 'Perplexity' and from 'Here and There'; Fadwa Tuqan, 'My Town', 'From a Prisoner's Diary in an Unknown Prison', 'I Shall Not Weep', 'Epiphany' and 'Last Wish'; Badr Shakir al-Sayyab, 'Rain Song' and 'The Book of Job'; Salah Abd al-Sabur, 'Abstractions', 'Fragments of a Common Tale' and 'Sumup'; Muhammad Afifi Matar, 'Recital'].

*Philip, Neil, ed., *War and the Pity of War* New York: Clarion Books, 1998 [Includes Sa'di Yusuf's poem 'Guns', Beirut, 1982].

*—— *It's a Woman's World: A Century of Women's Voices in Poetry* New York: Dutton Children's Books, 2000 [Includes Nazik al-Mala'ikah's poem 'Elegy for a Woman of No Importance'].

Pinter, Harold, Anthony Astbury and Geoffrey Godbert, eds, *99 Poems in Translation* London; Boston, MA: Faber and Faber, 1994 [Includes poems from other Near Eastern languages: Hebrew (five poems), Persian and Turkish (one poem each)].

Ragland, Cindy, ed., *International Portland Review 1980* Portland, OR: Publications Board, Portland State University, 1980 [An experimental multilingual anthology of poems presented in both original languages and in English translation. Scores of countries and languages from all continents are represented including Israel (Hebrew), Lebanon (a French poem by Salah Stétié) and Turkey (Turkish). No selections from Arabic poetry].

Rosenberg, Donna, ed., *World Literature: An Anthology of Great Short Stories, Drama and Poetry* Lincolnwood, IL: National Textbook Co., 1992 [Divided into six regions, the Mediterranean, Africa, the Far East, Latin America, North America and Great Britain – without including a single Arab writer].

*Rothenberg, Jerome, and Pierre Joris, eds, *Poems for the Millennium: The University of California Book of Modern & Postmodern Poetry.* Vol. 2 From Postwar to Millennium. Berkeley, CA: University of California Press, 1998 [Includes Adonis, from 'A Desire Moving through the Maps of the Material' and from 'Preface'; Mahmud Darwish, from 'Memory for Forgetfulness'; Unsi al-Haj, 'The Charlatan'; Yusuf al-Khal, 'Cain the Immortal' and 'The Wayfarers'; Muhammad al-Maghut, 'Executioner of Flowers'; and Badr Shakir al-Sayyab, 'The River and Death'].

*Rudnicki, Stefan, ed., *The Actor's Book of Monologues for Women from Non-Dramatic Sources* New York: Penguin Books, 1991 [Includes Nazik al-Mala'ikah, 'The Viper' and Fadwa Tuqan, 'Behind the Bars'].

*Schulte, Rainer, ed., *Contemporary Writing from the Continents* Athens, OH: Ohio University Press, 1981 [Includes poems by Adonis, Mahmud Darwish,

Unsi al-Haj, Jabra I. Jabra, Samih al-Oasim and Tawfiq Sayegh, in addition to other works written originally in English or French by Etel Adnan, Tahar Ben Jalloun, Andrée Chedid and Nadia Tueni].

Shields, Mike, ed., ORBIS *Century: 100 Major Modern Poets* Nuneaton, UK: ORBIS International Literary Quarterly, 1996 [Includes only a few non-English-speaking poets].

*Simpson, John, ed., *The Oxford Book of Exile* Oxford and New York: Oxford University Press, 1995 [Includes Salim Jubran, 'Singer of Wind and Rain', and Taha Abd al-Ghani Mustafa 'The Palestinian's Journey Home', in addition to prose passages by Salma Khadra Jayyusi and Amin Maalouf and an excerpt entitled 'The Prophet Mahomet Flees from Mecca to Medina' from Washington Irving's *The Life of the Prophet Mohammed* (1841)].

Steiner, George, ed.. *The Penguin Book of Modern Verse Translation* Harmondsworth, UK: Penguin Books, 1966 [Steiner left out translations from Persian and Arabic, stating, 'perhaps wrongly, I feel that those I have seen move in a saccharine limbo between the original and the natural shapes of English' (30)].

Tomlinson, Charles, ed., *The Oxford Book of Verse in English Translation* Oxford: Oxford University Press, 1980 [Includes a single pre-modern poet, Ibn Hazm al-Andalusi, mistakenly identified as Persian].

Troupe, Quincy, and Rainer Schulte, eds, *Giant Talk: An Anthology of Third World Writing* New York: Random House, 1975 [Limited to work by African, African–American and Latin American writers. Literatures from other developing countries are not represented].

Van Doren, Mark, ed., *An Anthology of World Poetry* New York: Albert & Charles Boni, 1928 [Includes about forty selections from classical Arabic poetry].

Voices: Poetry and Art from around the World, ed. Barbara Brenner. Washington, DC: National Geographic Society, 2000 [Includes Ahmad Abd al-Mu'ti Hijazi, 'Caption to a Landscape'].

Van Doren, Mark, and Garibaldi M. Lapolla, eds, *The World's Best Poems* New York: Albert & Charles Boni, 1929, 1932 [Includes some of the selections given in Van Doren's *Anthology of World Poetry*].

Washburn, Elizabeth, and John S. Major, eds, *World Poetry: An Anthology of Verse from Antiquity to our Time* New York: Norton, 1998 [Includes poets from the pre-Islamic and Andalusian periods only. The chapter on Arabic from pre-Islamic verse through the eleventh century (pp. 284–298) includes only pre-Islamic selections. There is nothing that belongs to the periods beyond the seventh century. As for the section on 'Hebrew and

Arabic Verse from Andalusian Spain and the Middle East', pp. 452–464, it is divided into equal sections for Hebrew (452–458) and Arabic (458–464). This attempt at 'equal representation' disregards the obvious fact that Arabic was the major literary language of the Andalusian period under survey].

*Willhardt, Mark, and Alan Michael Parker, eds, *Who's Who in Twentieth-Century World Poetry* London and New York: Routledge, 2000 [Includes brief entries about nineteen poets, listed in some cases without regard to the standard alphabetical order. Entries under A include 'Aql, al-Bayyati [Bayati], al-Jabal, Badawi [Badawi al-Jabal], al-Jawahiri, al-Mala'ikah, al-Sayyab, al-Shabbi, al-Tijani, Abdel-Sabur [Abd al-Sabur], Abu-Madi, Adunis. Other entries listed elsewhere cover Mahmud Darwish, Gibran, Hafiz Ibrahim [listed under Ibrahim, Hafiz], Ahmad Abd al-Mu'ti Hijazi, Nu'aima, Shawqi, Ali Mahmud Taha and Ibrahim Tuqan].

A Wrinkle in Time and Related Readings Evanston, IL: McDougal Littell, 1997 [Includes 'Behind the Bars' by Fadwa Tuqan].

Poets Represented in International Anthologies (marked with an asterisk):

Malak Abd al-Aziz 2

Jili Abd al-Rahman 1

Salah Abd al-Sabur 3

Fawziyya Abu Khalid 4

Ilya Abu Madi 1

Ahmad Zaki Abu Shadi 1

Muhammad Abu Sinna 1

Adonis 7

Abbas Mahmud al-Aqqad 4

Samar Attar 1

Badawi al-Jabal 1

Abd Allah al-Baradduni 1

Salim Barakat 1

Abd al-Wahhab al-Bayati 2

Mu'in Basisu 1

Sargon Boulus 1

Ali Darwish 1

Mahmud Darwish 12

Amal Dunqul 1

Muhammad al-Fituri 2

Muhammad al-Ghuzzi 1

Unsi al-Haj 1

Khalil Hawi 1

Buland al-Haydari 4

Ahmad Abd al-Mu'ti Hijazi 2

Rashid Husain 1

Fawaz Hussein 1

Mahmud Hasan Isma'il 1

Jabra I. Jabra 2

Abd al-Majid Ibn Jallun 1

Hatif Janabi 1

Nabil Janabi 1

Salih Jawdat 1

Salim Jubran 1

Fawzi Karim 1

Abd al-Karim Kassid 1

Yusuf al-Khal 4

Zabya Khamis 1

Nazih Khayr 1

Muhammad al-Maghut 3

Muhammad Mahjub 1

Ali al-Mak 1

Nazik al-Mala'ikah 8

Abd al-Aziz al-Maqalih 1

Muhammad Afifi Matar 2

Taha Abd al-Ghani Mustafa 1

Orkhan Muyassar 1

Abd al-Karim al-Na'im 1

Ibrahim Naji 1

Samih al-Qasim 1

Muhammad Qasim 1

Nizar Qabbani 2

Fu'ad Rifqa 2

Ma'ruf al-Rusafi 1

Su'ad al-Sabah 1

Radi Saduq 1

Saniyya Salih 1

Mona Sa'udi 1

Sadiq al-Sayigh 1

Tawfiq Sayigh 2

Yusuf Sayigh 1

Badr Shakir al-Sayyab 7

Abu al-Qasim al-Shabbi 1

Ahmad Shawqi 3

Yusif Bashir Tijani 1

Fadwa Tuqan 11

Ibrahim Tuqan 2

Sa'di Yusuf 2

Tawfiq Zayyad 1

As this list shows, the most frequently anthologized poets are Adonis (7 times), Mahmud Darwish (12), al-Mala'ikah (8), al-Sayyab (7) and Fadwa Tuqan (11).

CHAPTER SIX

Arabic Drama

Arabic drama is the least represented in English translation of all literary forms. This is due largely to its own peculiar and complex historical development as a new genre in Arabic.

Introduced first in Lebanon around the mid-nineteenth century, Arabic drama has had to overcome or cope with more obstacles than those experienced in the other genres: religious, social, political, literary and linguistic. Three of these have constantly preoccupied and in a sense beleaguered Arab playwrights in their creative efforts: the absence of a well-defined and developed dramatic tradition in Arabic; the linguistic dichotomy between the unified and unifying classical language on the one hand and the various naturally spoken varieties of Arabic labelled as dialects, colloquial speech and vernaculars; and the generally intolerant and often repressive political climate, which restricts the playwright's freedom to present his or her works to the public. The latter has contributed to the prevalent use of symbolism, folklore, historical events or figures and other dramatic tricks. This is why drama has undergone a long drawn-out process to emerge as a serious, respectable and authentic Arabic genre. Many writers have taken part in this process, from Marun al-Naqqash (Lebanon, 1817–1855), the first to introduce drama into Arabic, Abu Khalil al-Qabbani (Syria, 1833–1902), Ya'qub Sanu'/James Sanua (Egypt, 1839–1912), the leading neoclassical poet–dramatist Ahmad Shawqi (Egypt, 1868–1932) to Tawfiq al-Hakim (1898–1987) and the new generation of playwrights.

The most significant contribution of all came from al-Hakim, who was responsible, more than anyone else, for establishing Arabic drama on firm foundations. This he achieved through his remarkable and unmatched output of more than eighty plays and numerous expository writings in which he covered a broad range of dramatic types, themes and techniques. His masterly use of Classical Arabic as a dramatic medium has been widely acclaimed throughout the Arab world. al-Hakim epitomizes the Arab playwright's search for a suitable dramatic language; he used the colloquial in certain social plays and experimented, though only in one play, with the so-called 'third language', a language that conforms in writing to the rules of the classical but can be, with minor modifications, turned into the vernacular on the stage. His choice of the classical variety of Arabic in most of his plays reflects a keen awareness of the need to establish drama as an integral part of the unbroken literary tradition and as a truly pan-Arab genre capable of appealing to Arab audiences irrespective of their regional dialects.

Other Arab playwrights, particularly since the 1950s, have increasingly favoured the use of colloquial language in their works, for both stylistic and ideological reasons. Being the language spoken naturally in the home, in the street and in workplace, the colloquial is judged to be ideally suitable as an instrument of realistic presentation, characterization and immediate communication. There is no doubt that both intrinsic and external considerations favour the use of the colloquial, especially in comedies or plays dealing with the Arab people's political and social concerns. Nonetheless, the practice itself has its own drawbacks. It limits the play's chance of being appreciated or read as literature in the conventional sense. It may also lead to a new literary dichotomy in the form of sub-regional dramatic genres (Egyptian drama, Syrian drama, Iraqi drama, etc.) that differ not only from the pan-Arabic dramatic form but also from each other. Indeed, some of the same proponents of the colloquial, including one of its most dedicated practitioners, Yusuf Idris, have pointed to the difficulty of following plays staged in unfamiliar colloquial language.

Needless to say, the division of Arabic drama into two distinct types has presented the translators with a more onerous task, which demands, among other qualifications, competence not only in the standard classical language but also in one or more of its spoken variants. That is why only a few Western translators have been involved in the translation of colloquial plays in particular, as the Biliography indicates.

The English translations of Arabic drama in the present survey include five anthologies, three collections based on al-Hakim's writings and about twenty individual works representing Egyptian playwrights. Plays published in periodicals or in other general sources are not covered.

Abdel Wahab's *Modern Egyptian Drama* (1974) is intended to represent important trends of the Egyptian prose drama of the 1960s, which Abdel Wahab, as a drama critic, had frequently reviewed while in Egypt. It includes four plays by al-Hakim, Yusuf Idris, Mikha'il Ruman and Rashad Rushdi, all of which have as their central theme the struggle against power, and an excellent introduction. Manzalaoui's collection (1977) consists of nine plays, eight of which are by al-Hakim, Mahmud Taymur, Idris and other Egyptian playwrights. The ninth belongs to Muhammad Maghut, a leading Syrian novelist and poet. Only three of these plays (Maghut's and two by al-Hakim) are written originally in the classical language. Central among the features of this collection is the team approach followed in the process of translation, which involved in every case more than one translator. The overall stylistic revision was the responsibility of Andrew Parkin, a non-Arabist, a scholar of Western drama and poetry. According to his statements, Parkin's focus in his revisions was on speech for the stage, 'in the hope of making all the lines possible to deliver convincingly from stages in the English-speaking world'. Parkin's approach, meritorious as it is, cannot be assessed in view of the fact that the translations in this survey have rarely been staged in English-speaking countries.

Johnson-Davies's collection of *Egyptian One-Act Plays* (1981) presents five short plays written in the colloquial by al-Hakim, Alfred Farag, Ali Salim and two other lesser-known writers. Noted for his pioneering and leading role in translating modern Arabic literature since the 1940s, Johnson-Davies combines his fine translation with a brief introduction regarding Egypt's theatrical achievements, the need for more English translations and the artistic sophistication displayed in the works he selected as well as in the works of other authors, including Yusuf Idris and Nu'man 'Ashur. (Another anthology of *Egyptian One-Act Plays*, compiled by David Woodman, is noted below.)

The fourth, and undoubtedly broader in scope, is *Modern Arabic Drama* (1995), edited by Salma Khadra Jayyusi and Roger Allen. In an effort to present a pan-Arab view of contemporary Arabic drama and to complement earlier translations, Jayyusi and Allen chose twelve plays of varied lengths from the works of leading dramatists in several Arab countries: Egypt, Iraq, Kuwait, Lebanon, Palestine, Syria and Tunisia. Among the dramatists included are al-'Ani (Iraq), Ikhlasi (Syria), al-Madani (Tunisia), Mahfuz (Lebanon) and Wannus (Syria). This is in addition to four well-known Egyptian playwrights, Abd-al-Sabur, Diyab, Farag and Salim. Jayyusi's anthology continues the same team approach followed in her earlier works of translation from Arabic by enlisting a group of first and second translators. The latter include Alan Brownjohn, Richard Davies, Charles Doria and Desmond O'Grady. Apart from the preface written by the editors (Jayyusi and Allen), the anthology includes a detailed introduction written by M. M. Badawi in which he surveys the history of Arabic drama and discusses major authors (many of whom are not represented in the anthology) or dramatic trends in different parts of the Arab world.

The same observation applies in general to the fifth anthology edited by Jayyusi under the title *Short Arabic Plays: An Anthology* (2003). It presents twenty plays by sixteen noted playwrights from Egypt, Iraq, Jordan, Lebanon, Libya, Palestine, Syria and the United Arab Emirates. Varying in length, the plays are carefully chosen to represent not only the thematic richness of contemporary Arabic drama but also the diversity of dramatic techniques and forms Arab playwrights have skilfully tried out in their works. The plays reflect also the significant progress that Arab playwrights have made towards evolving a simplified dramatic language or 'a much quieter level of address, more akin to normal exchange', as Jayyusi suggests in her introduction. What is obviously missing in this anthology is a more adequate representation of or reference to works from other Arab countries, especially Morocco and Tunisia.

The three other collections of al-Hakim's plays by Hutchins (1981/1984) and Johnson-Davies (1973) cover various periods, themes and types (such as theatre of ideas and theatre of society) of al-Hakim's output from the 1930s to the 1970s. Hutchins's volumes include also selections from al-Hakim's introductory remarks or commentaries to his works.

Of all Arab playwrights, al-Hakim has received understandably the greatest attention in English, whether in translation or studies dedicated to his works. Perhaps thirty or more of his plays have been translated, most of which are included in all the collections cited above, with the exception of Jayyusi's, or have appeared as separate works. They include some of his best plays such as *The Tree Climber* (regarded as his masterpiece), translated by Johnson-Davies, and some of his earliest attempts in which he adapted Islamic material or themes, as in *The People of the Cave* (Cairo: 1989) and *Muhammad* (Cairo: 1985). An incomplete translation of the former was published earlier by P. J. Vatikiotis in the journal *The Islamic Literature* (1955, 1957). It is noteworthy that some of al-Hakim's plays are available in two or more translations. There are, for example, three versions of al-Hakim's full-length play *The Sultan's Dilemma*, as translated by Abdel-Wahab, M. M. Badawi in Manzalaoui's anthology and Johnson-Davies (1973), and two translations of a shorter play, *Song of Death*, by Badawi and Johnson-Davies.

Other important dramatists represented in the corpus are Salah Abd al-Sabur (1931–1981), Yusuf Idris (1927–1991) and Alfred Faraj (or Farag; 1929–). Abd al-Sabur is noted for his verse plays including *Murder in Baghdad* (a tragedy based on the martyrdom of al-Hallaj in Baghdad, 922, but highly relevant to the contemporary context) and *Night Traveller*, a black comedy pointing to man's helplessness in the face of tyranny. Idris, one of the greatest writers of fiction and drama, is highly acclaimed for his masterpiece *Farafir* (translated under the title of *Farfoors* by Abdel-Wahab and *Flipflap and his Master* by Trevor LeGassick, in Manzalaoui's anthology). A satirical but at the same time serious comedy, *Flipflap* stands out as a bold attempt not only to create a truly Egyptian drama based on Egypt's folkloric legacy but also to tackle a variety of interrelated local and universal themes of freedom, democracy, social injustice and the search for elusive absolute equality. Farag has written some of the finest politically oriented plays, based largely on adaptation of historical or folkloric materials from different periods. His comedy *'Ali Janah al-Tabrizi and his Servant Quffa* (which is included in Jayyusi's anthology but which appeared also as a book in Cairo, 1989) demonstrates his ability to create out of a tale from *The Arabian Nights* a work of considerable complexity and relevance. Aside from its comic presentation and its implications for the Arab world's realities, it raises, in Badawi's words, 'interesting questions such as the relation between illusion and reality [and] the thin line separating the prophet or social reformer from the impostor'.

We should not overlook other translations of Egyptian plays, which have been published in Cairo mostly by the General Egyptian Book Organization. Among the playwrights in the Organization's list are Abd al-Sabur, Farag, al-Hakim, Izz al-Din Isma'il, Samir Sarhan, Abd al-Rahman Sharqawi, and Sa'd al-Din Wahba.

As this brief survey indicates, modest progress has been made in recent years towards promoting the English translation of Arabic drama. Apart from the fact that only a limited number of plays have been translated, the translated texts have had, thus far, a marginal appeal beyond a narrow, largely Arabist, audience.

Bibliography

Anthologies and Collected Works

Arabic Writing Today: The Drama, ed. Mahmoud Manzalaoui. Cairo: The American Research Center in Egypt, 1977 [Includes Mahmud Taymur, *The Court Rules*; Tawfiq al-Hakim, *Song of Death* and *The Sultan's Dilemma*; Mahmud Diyab, *The Storm*; Shawqi Abd al-Hakim, *Hassan and Naima*; Yusuf Idris, *Flipflap and his Master*; Faruq Khurshid, *The Wines of Babylon*; Mikha'il Ruman, *The Newcomer*; and Muhammad al-Maghut, *The Hunchback Sparrow*].

Contemporary Theatre in Egypt, ed. Marvin Carlson. New York: The Graduate School and University Center, The City University of New York, c. 1999 [Includes Alfred Farag, *The Last Walk*, trans. Dina Amin; Gamal Maqsoud

[Jamal Abd al-Maqsud], *The Absent One*, trans. by the author; and Linin el-Ramli, *The Nightmare*, trans. Marvin Carlson and Wagdi Zeid].

Egyptian One-Act Plays, trans. Denys Johnson-Davies. London: Heinemann Educational Books, 1981 [Includes: Alfred Farag [Faraj], *The Trap*; Tawfiq al-Hakim, *The Donkey Market*; Farid Kamil, *The Interrogation*; Ali Salim, *The Wheat Well*; and Abd al-Mun'im Salim, *Marital Bliss*].

Egyptian One-Act Plays, compiled by David Woodman. Cairo: AUCP, 1974 [Published in two separate versions, Arabic and English, the anthology is based on the compiler's academic project at AUC to solicit one-act plays for possible staging at AUC's theatre. According to Woodman, a committee of prominent Egyptian scholars and writers (Suhayr al-Qalamawi, Hamdi Sakkut, Yahya Haqqi and Ahmad Zaki) participated in the selection of the plays].

Modern Arabic Drama: An Anthology, ed. Salma Khadra Jayyusi and Roger Allen. Introduction by M. M. Badawi. Bloomington, IN: Indiana University Press, 1995 [Includes Isam Mahfuz, *The China Tree*; Mamduh 'Udwan, *That's Life*; Sa'dallah Wannus, *The King Is the King*; Walid Ikhlasi, *The Path*; 'Izz al-Din al-Madani, *The Zanj Revolution*; The Balalin Company of Jerusalem, *Darkness*; Abd al-'Aziz al-Surayyi', *The Bird Has Flown*; Yusuf al-'Ani, *The Key*; Salah Abd al-Sabur, *Night Traveller*; Alfred Farag, *Ali Janah al- Tabrizi and his Servant Quffa*; Ali Salim, *The Comedy of Oedipus: You're the One Who Killed the Beast*; and Mahmud Diyab, *Strangers Don't Drink Coffee*].

Modern Egyptian Drama, trans. Farouk Abdel Wahab. Minneapolis, MN: Bibliotheca Islamica, 1974 [Includes Tawfiq al-Hakim, *The Sultan's Dilemma*; Mikha'il Ruman, *The New Arrival*; Rashad Rushdi, *A Journey outside the Wall*; and Yusuf Idris, *The Farfoors*].

Short Arabic Plays: An Anthology, ed. Salma Khadra Jayyusi. New York: Interlink Books, 2003 [Includes Yusuf al-'Ani, *Where the Power Lies*; Fatih Azzam and others, *Ansar*; Fateh Azzam, *Baggage*; Samia Qazmouz Bakri, *The Alley*; Mahmoud Diyab, *Men Have Heads*; Ahmad Ibrahim al-Fagih, *The Singing of the Stars*; Alfred Farag, *The Person*; Tawfiq al-Hakim, *Boss Kanduz's Apartment Building* and *War and Peace*; Jamal Abu Hamdan, *Actress J's Burial Night*; Walid Ikhlasi, *Pleasure Club 21*; Riad Ismat, *Was Dinner Good, Dear Sister?*; Raymond Jbara, *TheTraveller*; Sultan Ben Muhammad al-Qasimi, *The Return of Hulegu*; 'Ali Salim, *The Coffee Bar*; Mamdouh 'Udwan, *The Mask* and *Reflections of a Garbage Collector*; Sa'd al-Din Wahba, *The Height of Wisdom*; Sa'dallah Wannus, *The Glass Café* and *The King's Elephant*].

Individual Works

'Abd al-Maqsud, Jamal, *The Man Who Ate a Goose*, trans. Atef al-Sayed. Cairo: GEBO, 1991.

'Abd al-Sabur, Salah, *Murder in Baghdad*, trans. Khalil Semaan. Leiden: E. J. Brill, 1972; Cairo: GEBO, 1976.

—— *Leila and the Madman*, trans. M. M. Enani. Cairo: Ministry of Culture, Foreign Cultural Relations, in cooperation with the Supreme Council for Culture, 1999.

—— *Night Traveller*, trans. M. M. Enani. Cairo: GEBO, 1980.

—— *Now the King is Dead*, trans. Nehad Selaiha. Cairo: GEBO, 1986.

—— *The Princess Waits*, trans. Shafik Megally. Cairo: GEBO, 1975.

'Ashur, Nu'man, *Give us our Money Back*, trans. Mahmoud El Lozy. Cairo: Elias Modern Publishing House, 1994.

—— *The House of al-Dughry*, trans. Mohamed Abd al-Atty. Revised by Wagdi Zeid. Cairo: Ministry of Culture, Foreign Cultural Relations, 1998.

Bashir, Abd Allah al-Shaykh Muhammad, *When the Eagle Dreams*, trans. unknown. Cairo: GEBO, 1996.

Diyab, Mahmud, *Bab al-Futuh 'Gate to Conquest'*, trans. Fatma Moussa Mahmoud and Amal Aly Mazhar. Cairo: GEBO, 1999.

Enani, see Inani.

Faqih, Ahmad Ibrahim, *Gazelles and Other Plays* London: Kegan Paul, 2000

Faraj [also known as Farag], Alfred *The Caravan, or Ali Janah al-Tabrizi and his Servant Quffa*, trans. Rasheed el-Enany. Cairo: GEBO, 1989.

—— *Marriage by Decree Nisi*, trans. Ken Whittingham. Cairo: GEBO, 1992.

—— *Al-Zear Salim*, trans. Khadija Allak. Cairo: GEBO, 1995.

al-Hakim, Tawfiq, *A Conversation with the Planet Earth* and *The World Is a Comedy*, trans. Riad Habib Youssef. Cairo: GEBO, 1985.

—— *The Donkey Market*, trans. Roger Allen. *The Arab World* October–February 1971–72: 20-28. Reprinted in *Small Planet*, ed. B. Stanford and Gene Stanford. New York: Harcourt Brace Jovanovich, 1975: 70–81.

—— *Fate of a Cockroach: Four Plays of Freedom*, trans. Denys Johnson-Davies. London: Heinemann, 1973 [Includes *Fate of a Cockroach*, *The Song of Death*, *The Sultan's Dilemma* and *Not a Thing out of Place*].

—— *Muhammad*, trans. Ibrahim Hassan el-Mougy. Revised by William M. Hutchins. Cairo: Al-Adab Press, 1985.

—— *The People of the Cave*, trans. Mahmoud El Lozy. Cairo: Elias Modern Publishing House, 1989.

—— *Plays, Prefaces, and Postscripts*. 2 vols, trans. William M. Hutchins. Washington, DC: Three Continents Press, 1981–1984 [Vol. I, entitled *Theater of the Mind*, includes *The Wisdom of Solomon*, *King Oedipus*, *Shahrazad*, *Princess Sunshine* and *Angels' Prayer*. Vol. II, *Theater of Society*, includes *Between War and Peace*, *Tender Hands*, *Food for the Millions*, *Poet on the Moon*, *Incrimination* and *Voyage to Tomorrow*].

—— *The Tree Climber*, trans. Denys Johnson-Davies. London: Oxford University Press, 1966. Second edition. London: Heinemann; Washington, DC: Three Continents Press, 1985.

Inani, Muhammad Muhammad, *The Prisoner and the Jailor*, trans. Nayla Naguib. Cairo: GEBO, 1989.

Isma'il, Izz-el-Din, *The Trial of an Unknown Man (A Poetic Drama)*, trans. M. M. Enani. Cairo: GEBO, 1985.

Jad, Nihad, *Adila and the Bus Stop*, trans. Angele Botros Samaan. Cairo: GEBO, 1987.

Juwaydah, Faruq, *Blood Stains on the Veils of the Kaaba*, trans. Suad Mahmoud Naguib. Cairo: GEBO, 1996.

—— *The Fall of Cordova*, trans. M. M. Enani. Cairo: GEBO, 1988.

Mahfuz, Najib, *One-Act Plays*, trans. Nehad Selaiha. Cairo: GEBO, 1989.

el-Ramli, Linin, *In Plain Arabic*, trans. Esmet Allouba. Cairo: AUCP, 1994.

—— *A Point of View*, trans. Yussif Hifnawi. Revised by Wagdi Zeid. Cairo: Ministry of Culture, Foreign Cultural Information Department, 1999.

Rushdi, Rashad, *Five Egyptian One-Act Plays* Cairo: Anglo-Egyptian Bookshop, c. 1955 [According to the author, the five plays – *A Liar*, *Odysseus*, *The Plague*, *At Home* and *Sinhue* – were performed during 1951 and 1952].

Salamuni, Muhammad Abu al-'Ula, *Revenge: Quest of Pain*, trans. Fatma Moussa Mahmoud and Mohammed El-Guindy. Cairo: Ministry of Culture, Foreign Cultural Relations: The Supreme Council for Culture, 1999.

Salim, Ali, *The Buffet and the Well of Wheat*, trans. John Waterbury. Cairo: GEBO, 1991.

—— *The Buffet*, trans. John Waterbury. *American Universities Fieldstaff Reports* (Northeast African Series) No. 18 (March 1973): 1–19.

—— *The Well of Wheat*, trans. John Waterbury. *Ibid.* No. 19 (May 1974): 1–18.

—— *Dogs Reached the Airport*, trans. Rachel Cranton. Cairo: GEBO, 1997.

—— *Oedipus: You, Who Killed the Beast,* trans. John Waterbury. Cairo: GEBO, 1997.

Sarhan, Samir, *The Lady on the Throne,* trans. Mona Mikhail. Cairo: GEBO, 1989.

Salamawi, Muhammad, *Come Back Tomorrow and Other Plays,* trans. William M. Hutchins. Cairo: Alef Publishing House; Washington, DC: Three Continents Press, 1984.

—— *Two down the Drain,* trans. Roland Trafford-Roberts. Cairo: GEBO, 1993.

Sharqawi, Abd al-Rahman, *Husayn the Martyr: A Play in Six Scenes,* trans. Anam Abdul-Razzaq. Chicago: The Open School, 1997 [Described by the translator as 'a free translation of the play']. Second edition, 2003.

—— *Orabi Leader of the Fellahin. A Verse Translation,* trans. Thoraya Mahdi Allam. Revised by M. Mahdi Allam. Cairo: GEBO, 1989.

Shawqi, Ahmad, *Majnun Layla,* trans. A. J. Arberry. Cairo: Dar al-Maarif, 1933.

—— *Quais and Laila* [*Majnun Laila*], trans. Jeanette W. S. Atiya. Cairo: GEBO, 1990.

Wahba, Sa'd al-Din, *Mosquito Bridge,* trans. Charlotte Shabrawi. Revised by Samir Sarhan. Cairo: GEBO, 1987.

—— *The Road of Safety,* trans. Fawzi M. Tadros and Patricia A. Kinchlow. Cairo: GEBO, 1979.

Wannus, Sa'dallah, *Sahrah ma'a Abi Khalil al-Qabbani,* trans. Shawkat M. Toorawa. *Arabic and Middle Eastern Literatures* Online. 3.1 (2000).

—— *The Elephant, Oh Lord of Ages,* trans. Peter Clark. *Arabic and Middle Eastern Literatures* Online. 4.1 (2003).

Zayn al-Din, Abd al-Sami' 'Umar, *The Sultan's Good Morrow: A One-Act Play in Verse* Cairo: GEBO. 1992.

Further Reading

Allen, Roger, ed., *Critical Perspectives on Yusuf Idris* Colorado Springs, CO: Three Continents Press, 1994.

—— *An Introduction to Arabic Literature* Cambridge, UK and New York: Cambridge University Press, 2000.

An Anthology of Non-Western Drama, ed. Ali Kiani. Lido Beach, NY: Whittier Publications, 1993 [Includes Tawfiq al-Hakim's *The Sultan's Dilemma* as translated by Farouk Abdel Wahab, pp. 383–492].

Badawi, M. M., *Modern Arabic Drama in Egypt* Cambridge: Cambridge University Press, 1987.

—— ed., *Modern Arabic Literature* Cambridge, UK: Cambridge University Press, 1992.

Contemporary Theatre in Egypt, ed. Marvin Carlson. New York: The Graduate School and University Center, The City University of New York, c. 1999 [Includes the proceedings of the February 1999 Symposium held at The City University of New York on contemporary Egyptian theatre and the three plays cited in the bibliography above under the same title].

Hutchins, William W., *Tawfiq al-Hakim: A Reader's Guide* Boulder, CO: Lynne Rienner, 2003.

Machut-Mendecka, Ewa, *The Art of Arabic Drama: A Study in Typology,* trans. from the Polish by Teresa Opalinska. Warsaw: Dialog, 1997.

—— *Studies in Arabic Theatre and Literature* Warsaw: Dialog, 2000: 12–113.

Meserve, Walter, 'Some Observations on Modern Egyptian Drama' *al-'Arabiyya* 9 (1976): 45–51.

Moreh, Shmuel and Philip Sadgrove, *Jewish Contributions to Nineteenth-Century Arabic Theatre: Plays from Algeria and Syria* Oxford: Oxford University Press, 1996.

Sulayhah, Nihad [also known as Selaiha, Nehad], *Egyptian Theatre: A Diary 1990–1992* Cairo: GEBO, 1993.

Udnicka-Kassem, Dorota, *Egyptian Drama and Social Change: A Study of Thematic and Artistic Development in Yusuf Idris's Plays* Cracow and Montreal: Enigma Press, 1993.

The World Encyclopedia of Contemporary Theatre. Vol. 4. The Arab World, ed. Don Rubin. London and New York: Routledge, 1994.

Zuhur, Sherifa, ed., *Colors of Enchantment: Theatre, Dance, Music, and the Visual Arts of the Middle East* Cairo: AUCP, 2001.

Literary Autobiographies and Memoirs[1]

Afifi, Muhammad, *Little Songs in the Shade of Tamaara*, trans. Lisa White. Fayetteville, AR: University of Arkansas Press, 2000.

Attar, Samar, 'To Create and in Creating to Be Created': Reflections on the Mixing of Fiction and Memoir in *Lina: A Portrait of a Damascene Girl* and *The House of Arnus Square*', in *Auto/Biography and the Construction of Identity and Community in the Middle East*, ed. Mary Ann Fay. New York: Palgrave, 2001: 215–226 [Attar reflects on her own novels published in 1994 and 1998].

Barghouti, Mourid, *I Saw Ramallah*, trans. Ahdaf Soueif. Cairo: AUCP, 2000.

Basisu, Mu'in, *Descent into the Water: Palestinian Notes from Arab Exile*, trans. Saleh Omar. Wilmette, IL: The Medina Press, 1980.

Darwish, Mahmud, M*emory for Forgetfulness: August, Beirut*, trans. Ibrahim Muhawi. Berkeley, CA: University of Berkeley Press, 1995.

Faqir, Fadia, ed., *In the House of Silence: Autobiographical Essays by Arab Women Writers*, trans. Shirley and Fadia Faqir. Reading, UK: Garnet, 1998 [Thirteen Arab women novelists reflect on their mostly painful experience as they struggle to assert their role and independence in a traditional patriarchal culture. The authors selected for this collection represent several Arab countries: Liyanah Badr (Palestine), Salwa Bakr (Egypt), Hoda Barakat (Lebanon), Fadia Faqir (Jordan), Samira al-Mana' and Alia Mamdouh (both

---

1. As stated in the Introduction, the term 'literary' or 'belletristic' is used here in a narrow sense to specifically refer to diverse accounts written by poets, novelists and playwrights. This list is a preliminary attempt to identify English translations of such accounts, as well as selected relevant studies. I have included several recent interviews with leading Arab novelists and poets, because they include illuminating autobiographical information as well as views on the translation of Arabic literature.

from Iraq), Ahlem Mosteghanemi (Algeria), Arousia Nalouti ['Arusiyya al-Natuli] (Tunisia), Hamidah Na'na' (Palestine), Zhor Ounissi [Zuhur Wannisi] (Algeria), Fawziya Rashid (Bahrain), Nawal al-Sa'dawi (Egypt) and Hadia Said (Lebanon)].

al-Hakim, Tawfiq, *The Prison of Life: An Autobiographical Essay*, trans. Pierre Cachia. Cairo: AUCP, 1992.

—— *My Parents*, trans. Pierre Cachia. Cairo: AUCP, 1997 [Extract from *The Prison of Life: An Autobiographical Essay* cited earlier].

Husayn, Taha, *An Egyptian Childhood*, trans. E. H. Paxton. London: 1932; London: Heinemann; Washington, DC: Three Continents Press, 1981; Cairo; AUCP, 1990.

—— *A Passage to France*, trans. Kenneth Cragg. Leiden: E. J. Brill, 1976.

—— *The Stream of Days*, trans. Hilary Wayment. Cairo: Dar al-Ma'arif, 1943; London and New York: Longman, Green, 1948.

Jabra, Jabra I., *The First Well: A Bethlehem Boyhood*, trans. Issa J. Boullata. Fayetteville, AR: University of Arkansas Press, 1995.

Kamil, Mahmud, *Diary of an Egyptian Lawyer: The Human Side of a Court of Law* Cairo: GEBO, 1980.

Mahfuz, Najib, *Echoes of an Autobiography*, trans. Denys Johnson-Davies. New York: Doubleday, 1997.

Munif, Abdelrahman, *Story of a City: A Childhood in Amman*, trans. Samira Kawar. London: Quartet Books, 1998.

al-Qusaybi, Ghazi Abd al-Rahman, *Yes, (Saudi) Minister: A Life in Administration* London: London Centre of Arab Studies, 1999.

al-Sa'dawi, Nawal, *Memoirs from the Women's Prison*, trans. Marilyn Booth. London: The Women's Press, 1986.

—— *A Daughter of Isis: The Autobiography of Nawal El Saadawi*, trans. Sherif Hetata. London: Zed Books, 1999.

—— *Walking Through Fire: A Life of Nawal El Saadawi*, trans. Sherif Hetata. London: Zed Books, 2002.

Tuqan, Fadwa, *A Mountainous Journey, a Difficult Journey: The Life of Palestine's Outstanding Woman Poet*, trans. Olive Kenny. London: The Women's Press, 1990. See also 'Difficult Journey–Mountainous Journey' translated by Donna Robinson Divine in *Opening the Gates: A Century of Arab Feminist Writing*, ed. Margot Badran and Miriam Cooke. Bloomington, IN: Indiana University Press, 1990: 26–41, which first appeared in 1984 in *The Female Autograph*, ed. Donna C. Stanton, New York: New York Literary Forum,

1984: 213–233; then in the revised edition of the same title and editor, Chicago, IL: University of Chicago Press, 1987: 187–204.

Selected Interviews

Adonis, 'An Interview with Adonis' by Margaret Obank and Samuel Shimon. *Banipal* 2 (June 1998): 30–39.

Algosaibi, Ghazi, 'Interview' by Margaret Obank. *Banipal* 5 (Summer 1999): 16–19.

Ashour, Radwa, 'My Experience with Writing'. *The View from Within: Writers and Critics on Contemporary Arabic Literature*, eds Ferial J. Ghazoul and Barbara Harlow. Cairo: AUCP, 1994: 7–11.

Beydhoun [Baydun], Abbas, 'Interview' by Camilo Gomez-Riva. *Banipal* 10/11 (Spring/Summer 2001): 32–38.

Boulus, Sargon, 'Interview' by Margaret Obank. *Banipal* 1 (February 1998): 8–18.

Da'if, Rashid, 'Interview' by Margaret Obank. *Banipal* 6 (Autumn 1999): 48–59.

Darwish, Mahmud, 'Interview', trans. Ibrahim Muhawi. *Banipal* 4 (Spring 1999): 5–11 [Based on an interview with the Tunisian writer Hassouna Mosbahi, published originally in Arabic in *al-Majallah*, London].

Ghallab, Abdelkarim (Abd al-Karim) [Interview with], 'My Autobiographical Experience'. *Remembering for Tomorrow* Toledo: European Cultural Foundation and Escuela de Traduxtores de Toledo: 59–63 [One of the most important Moroccan novelists, Ghallab briefly comments on four of his autobiographical novels/works: *Seven Doors, The Book of Formation, An Unjust Old Age* and *Cairo Reveals its Secrets*].

al-Ghitani, Jamal, 'Intertextual Dialectics'. *The View from Within: Writers and Critics on Contemporary Arabic Literature*, eds Ferial J. Ghazoul and Barbara Harlow. Cairo: AUCP, 1994: 17–26.

—— 'Interview' by Nabil Sharaf el-Din. *Banipal* 13 (Spring 2000): 8–13.

al-Kharrat, Edwar, 'Interview' by Margaret Obank. *Banipal* 6 (Autumn 1999): 31–33.

Khuri, Ilyas, 'Interview' by Sonja Mejcher. *Banipal* 12 (Autumn 2001): 8–14.

Munif, Abdelrahman, 'Interview' by Samuel Shimon. *Banipal* 3 (Autumn 1998): 8–14.

Salih, Tayeb, 'Interview' by Mohammed Shaheen. *Banipal* 10/11 (Spring/Summer 2001): 82–84.

Tayeb Salih Speaks: Four Interviews with the Sudanese Novelist, trans. and ed. Constance E. Berkley and Osman Hassan Ahmed, Washington, DC: Embassy of the Sudan, Office of the Cultural Counsellor, 1982. [According to the translators, the interviews were published in *al-Anba'*, Kuwait, 10 January 1978; *al-Fajr*, Doha, Qatar, 15 November 1976; *al-A yyam*, Khartoum, Sudan, 28 October, 4 and 11 November 1977, in addition to a taped interview broadcast by the 'Voice of the Arabs', date not known.]

al-Zayyat, Latifah, 'On Political Commitment and Feminist Writing'. *The View from Within: Writers and Critics on Contemporary Arabic Literature*, eds Ferial J. Ghazoul and Barbara Harlow. Cairo: AUCP, 1994: 244–260.

Studies

Note: OW = Ostle, Robin et al., eds, *Writing the Self: Autobiographical Writing in Modern Arabic Literature* London: Saqi, 1998.

Aghacy, Samira, 'The use of Autobiography in Rashid al-Da'if's *Dear Mr Kawabata*'. *OW*: 217–228 and 321–323.

Allen, Roger, 'Autobiography and Memory: Mahfuz's Asda' al-sira al-dhatiyya'. *OW*: 207–216 and 319–321.

Bennett, Sophie, 'A Life of One's Own?'. *OW*: 283–291 and 329–332 [Latifah al-Zayyat].

Calvert, John, 'The Individual and the Nation: Sayyid Qutb's *Tifl min al-qarya* (Child from the Village)'. *Muslim World* 90.1–2 (2000): 108–134.

Corrao, Francesca Maria, 'The Autobiography of the Thief of Fire by Abd al-Wahhab al-Bayyati [Bayati]'. *OW*: 241–248 and 324–325.

el-Enany, Rasheed, 'The Promethean Quest in Louis 'Awad's *Memoirs of an Overseas Student*'. *OW*: 61–71 and 297–298.

Gabrieli, Francesco, 'The Autobiography of Mikhaail Nu'aima'. *Islam and its Cultural Divergence: Studies in Honor of Gustav E. von Grunebaum*, ed. Girdhari Tikku. Urbana, IL: University of Illinois Press, 1971: 52–62.

Gonzalez-Quijano, Yves, 'The Territory of Autobiography: Mahmud Darwish's *Memory for Forgetfulness*', trans. from the French by Hannah Davis. *OW*: 183–191 and 317–318.

Malti-Douglas, Fadwa, *Blindness and Autobiography: Al-Ayyam of Taha* Husayn. Princeton, NJ: Princeton University Press, 1988.

Manisty, Dinah, 'Negotiating the Space between Private and Public: Women's Autobiographical Writing in Egypt'. *OW*: 272–282 and 328– 329 [Discusses Nawal al-Sa'dawi, Latifah al-Zayyat, Salwa Bakr and Sakinah Fu'ad].

Moor, Ed de, 'Autobiography, Theory and Practice: The Case of *al-Ayyam*'. *OW*: 128–138 and 307–308.

Neuwirth, Angelika, 'Jabra Ibrahim Jabra's Autobiography, *al-Bi'r al-ula*, and his Concept of a Celebration of Life'. *OW*: 115–127 and 303–307.

al-Nowaihi, Magda, 'Resisting Silence in Arab Women's Autobiographies'. *International Journal of Middle Eastern Studies* 33.4 (2001): 477–502 [Deals with Fadwa Tuqan's *A Mountainous Journey*, Assia Djebar's *Fantasia* and Latifah Zayyat's *The Search*].

Odeh, Nadja, 'Coded Emotions: The Description of Nature in Arab Women's Autobiographies'. *OW*: 263–271 and 327–328 [Huda Sha'rawi and Fadwa Tuqan].

Ostle, Robin et al., eds, *Writing the Self: Autobiographical Writing in Modern Arabic Literature* London: Saqi, 1998.

Reynolds, Dwight F., ed., *Interpreting the Self: Autobiography in the Arabic Literary Tradition* Berkeley, CA: University of California Press, 2001 [An important source on Arabic autobiographies written prior to the twentieth century. It includes a brief discussion of an autobiographical introduction, which Ahmad Shawqi (1968–1932) wrote for his 1898 *diwan*. The book concludes with a useful annotated guide to autobiographies, including the works of several twentieth-century writers such as Ahmad Shawqi, Abd al-Rahman Shukri and Taha Husayn].

Rooke, Tetz, *In My Childhood: A Study of Arabic Autobiography* Stockholm: Stockholm University, 1997.

—— 'The Arabic Autobiography of Childhood'. *OW*: 100–111 and 301–303.

—— 'The Influence of *Adab* on the Muslim Intellectuals of the *nahda* as Reflected in the Memoirs of Muhammad Kurd 'Ali (1876–1953)' [A paper given at the Oslo conference of The Middle East in Globalizing World, August 1998]. See the printed version in *The Middle East in a Globalized World*, ed. Olav Utvik and Knut S. Vikør. Bergen: Nordic Society for Middle Eastern Studies, 2000: 193–219.

Shuiski, Sergei A., 'Some Observations on Modern Arabic Autobiography'. *Journal of Arabic Literature* 13 (1992).

Walther, Wiebke, 'My Hands Assisted the Hands of Events': The Memoirs of the Iraqi Poet Muhammad Mahdi al-Jawahiri'. *OW*: 249–232 and 325–327 [Dhikrayat, 2 vols, 1988, 1991].

Wild, Stefan, 'Nizar Qabbani's Autobiography: Images of Sexuality, Death, and Poetry'. *Love and Sexuality in Modern Arabic Literature*, ed. Roger Allen, Hilary Kilpatrick and Ed de Moor. London: Saqi, 1995: 200–209.

—— 'Searching for Beginnings in Modern Arabic Autobiography'. *OW*: 82–99 and 299–301.